MW01017078

THE I OF GOD

From Chaos to Creation

JUDITH ATTFIELD

BALBOA.
PRESS

A DIVISION OF HAY HOUSE

Copyright © 2017 Judith Attfield.

All rights reserved. No part of this book may be used or reproduced by any means, graphic, electronic, or mechanical, including photocopying, recording, taping or by any information storage retrieval system without the written permission of the author except in the case of brief quotations embodied in critical articles and reviews.

Balboa Press books may be ordered through booksellers or by contacting:

Balboa Press
A Division of Hay House
1663 Liberty Drive
Bloomington, IN 47403
www.balboapress.com
1 (877) 407-4847

Because of the dynamic nature of the Internet, any web addresses or links contained in this book may have changed since publication and may no longer be valid. The views expressed in this work are solely those of the author and do not necessarily reflect the views of the publisher, and the publisher hereby disclaims any responsibility for them.

The author of this book does not dispense medical advice or prescribe the use of any technique as a form of treatment for physical, emotional, or medical problems without the advice of a physician, either directly or indirectly. The intent of the author is only to offer information of a general nature to help you in your quest for emotional and spiritual well-being. In the event you use any of the information in this book for yourself, which is your constitutional right, the author and the publisher assume no responsibility for your actions.

Any people depicted in stock imagery provided by Thinkstock are models, and such images are being used for illustrative purposes only.
Certain stock imagery © Thinkstock.

Print information available on the last page.

ISBN: 978-1-5043-9207-5 (sc)
ISBN: 978-1-5043-9209-9 (hc)
ISBN: 978-1-5043-9208-2 (e)

Library of Congress Control Number: 2017918086

Balboa Press rev. date: 12/07/2017

DEDICATION

This book is dedicated to those who are suffering and wish to find peace.

This book is dedicated to those who want to find compassion, kindness and love in the world.

This book is dedicated to those who want to be a living, breathing, creative force in their lives.

This book is for those who are suffering and want to be
a living, breathing, creative force in their lives.

TABLE OF CONTENTS

ACKNOWLEDGEMENTS

I could not have written this book without the help of other people and I am grateful to them. To my husband, Ray Attfield, thank you for your support, encouragement, humungous hours of discussion and love. Without you, this book could not have been written. Thank you to my friends, Catherine Temple, Pauline Wolf and Suzan Badgley (the Geko Treker) for the years of philosophical discussion and your belief in me to write this book. Thank you to my sisters, Johanna Clark and Janice Kovacs, and to my daughter, Lillooet Wasilenkoff, for your love, encouragement and support. Thank you to Ryan Orbell from Hay House Publishing. Your patience and willingness to work with me gave me the courage to finish my book. Thank you to my copy editor, Trevor McMonagle, for your enthusiasm and care of my book. You helped me take my book to the next level. Without all of you, *The I of God* would not have been possible.

FOREWORD

When I began writing this book, I believed that God was the supreme creator and I was the supplicant trying to feel some sense of connection or spirituality *to* Him. As time went on and I continued to write, I began to understand that not only was there no God out there, God was not as I perceived it to be. That was very difficult for me to understand as I had always felt that if I could be good enough, or spiritually inclined, one day I would feel God. I had thought that if I were perfect enough God would reward me and I would be happy and prosperous forever.

In writing this book, I have become convinced that each of us can speak to god whenever we want to because we are god. We have always felt the force of our nature but have shied away from owning our part of it. From the beginning, we have created gods rather than accepting our responsibility for our creations.

My friend, Suzan, asked a monk, "If everything is god, are mosquitoes god too?" The monk replied: "Of course mosquitoes are god." Suzan then asked:" Since mosquitoes are god, is it okay that we kill them?" The monk replied: "If you love mosquitoes, you can get along with them and perhaps they wouldn't bite you." She observed him for a while and noticed that while mosquitoes hovered around him, they didn't land.

We are god and so is everything else. There is no separation between god and us. God is everything including mosquitoes and we can become aware of this.

Our ability to create beliefs and stories is part of our divinity. We have not been trained to be responsible creators and so we create gods outside of ourselves. This is why we yearn for the experience of oneness or enlightenment. We feel an integral part of us is missing.

We don't need to follow a spiritual path, become a vegetarian, meditate, do yoga or chant mantras. Being god cannot be changed. It is who we are and when we believe it, we understand that we are not connected to god, we are the god connection.

If you find the term god offensive to your beliefs, please feel free to use any similar term such as universe, energy, all that is, luck or higher self. As we go along, you may find it simpler to just say god.

There is no such thing as enlightenment. There is only the lifting of illusion.

A good tomorrow-worry story is about having to live under a bridge, where the final worry may go like this, "I will lie under the bridge alone and unloved and when I die nobody will care."

In the Beginning

E ver since man first looked up into the night sky, the mystery of life has permeated his being. To early tribes, life seemed precarious because death and tomorrow were unknown. They balanced their fears with religious rituals and ceremonies to help themselves, their friends and their relatives live life and move on to the next world.

The first known religious practice was with Paleolithic[1] man around fifty thousand years ago. Intentional graves containing food, tools, pottery and stone were discovered. To this day, we bury our dead with grave goods as part of our funeral rituals. Imagine how many generations of people it has been who use burials as a religious ceremony in order to help our loved ones into the next world.

Our ancient ancestors asked for guidance and divine intervention to help keep them safe in their daily lives. They believed that as long as they revered their gods and followed the rules, morning would come and they would still be alive.

Here is an example of an old prayer that we still use, asking god to help us survive the night.

> Now I lay me down to sleep,
> I pray the Lord my soul to keep,
> If I should die before I wake,
> I pray the Lord my soul to take.[2]

---

[1] Wikipedia. 2015. Paleolithic Religion. Last modified February 8, 2017. https://en.wikipedia.org/wiki/Paleolithic_religion

[2] Wikipedia. 2015. Now I Lay Me Down To Sleep. Last modified January 16, 2017. https://en.wikipedia.org/wiki/Now_I_Lay_Me_Down_to_Sleep

This prayer is at least four hundred years old. Even then, the fear of death was prominent. Today we still feel powerless in the face of death and tomorrow.

Since early times, many philosophers, shamans, scholars and scientists have tried to answer the mystery of life and death including whether or not god exists. They asked, "Why aren't we satisfied with our lives? What is life anyway? What is god? Is it instinct? Is it a belief?"

There have been many philosophies and religions created that have tried to answer these questions. Philosophers and theologians sought understanding about life so that we could feel safe and secure and live our lives in peace.

We are afraid that we will not be able to complete our lives or fulfill our dreams before destruction or death comes knocking at our doors. We don't know how to reach our potential because we are steered toward employment and lifestyle choices that suit our society's needs. We don't understand how to think outside the box of rules of how to be human. Yet, the desire for self-fulfillment is one of our drives.

Freda was just such a person. She had had a full life. She raised her children. She worked at a nursing care job. She was married to a great guy. She retired to watch her grandchildren grow up and be successful in the world. At ninety-three when she was dying, she was furious that she hadn't completed her life. She felt she had missed out, not paid attention to her yearning for fullness, for that connection with life and she had no idea what death was going to present to her.

Abraham Maslow[3] was a psychologist from the 1970's who developed a theory on our need to be fulfilled and to feel complete. He created a hierarchy of those needs and described them as a pyramid with our base needs on the bottom leading to the peak of self-development.

Maslow described our *physiological needs* as basic survival requirements. These are having enough food to eat, water to drink, clothing, shelter and procreation.

---

[3] Wikipedia. 2017. Maslow's hierarchy of needs. Last modified March 20, 2017. https://en.wikipedia.org/wiki/Maslow%27s_hierarchy_of_needs

Yet, some homeless people choose to deny themselves some of these needs. They believe that their freedom from our social rules is more important than their survival. Buddhist monks beg for food on the streets. They believe it builds humility and creates merits in this lifetime. It appears that we can shape what our base needs are, from our beliefs.

Our *safety needs* relate to our sense of security. We feel better if we can plan for tomorrow by having enough money and perhaps some insurance. Living in a country safe from war can also help. PTSD or post-traumatic stress disorder can destroy that sense of safety. This can occur with rape, war, financial destruction, death of a close loved one or childhood abuse.

We don't understand why we keep worrying when we tell ourselves not to. Perhaps that is a key to being ourselves. If we felt that we belong here, no matter what our situation, perhaps our lives would be different.

Our sense of community and a happy family life fulfill our need for *love and belonging.*

Without that sense of belonging to society, we can feel crippled, isolated, alone and/or suicidal.

Ostracism is used as a form of punishment to keep us in line with cultural values. We fear judgment and can lose belief in ourselves as being important in life.

Esteem, including self-esteem, is our next basic need for us to feel self-confident, capable and strong. Without esteem in our lives from both others and ourselves, we can feel inferior, self-doubting and helpless.

From the time we are born, we are told who we are by our family, friends, educators and governments. We are called immature, consumers, parishioners, and taxpayers. Somehow our personhood is not included.

After observing the behaviour of Mother Teresa, Eleanor Roosevelt and other self-made people, Maslow added a fifth level to his theory of needs, which he described as *self-actualization.* He said that to reach this level, one had to master all of the other needs first. In other words, we first have to feel safe, comfortable with ourselves and secure in our lives before we have the drive towards self-fulfillment. This is the desire to be all that we can be, whether it is the child that needs to be loved, the picture that needs to be painted, the book that needs to be written or the race that needs to be won. It is what our lives demand of us to feel fulfilled in the world.

If we accept this as a self-evident truth, why don't we learn this in school? Imagine feeling safe, secure and free in this world, no matter what our skin colour is, our choice of religion is, or what our gender is. We would require confidence in ourselves and our world for us to feel safe and secure.

In 1971, Maslow added a need that he called self-transcendence. This need is the yearning towards togetherness or wholeness. It is the drive towards oneness which *includes the divine.*

It turns out that our human race feels a oneness in god. For the last ten thousand years of recorded history we have written about our gods and how they help us and guide us with moral principles. We have fashioned our gods after ourselves. For example, in our society today, Gaia is the loving mother, Yahweh is the disciplining father and Jesus is the beloved son. Just as in the days of the ancient Greeks and Romans, our present-day gods represent our characteristics.

According to Steven Levine, our need for self-transcendence is our homesickness for god. It is what creates our sense of emptiness in our darkest hours. It is the cry in the night and the struggle in the face of great tragedy.[4]

In our everyday life there is no place for the divine because we believe god is about going to church and listening to someone telling us how to behave. In today's world the struggle to placate, embrace, accept or deny god still haunts us.

The three main monotheistic religions - Judaism, Christianity and Islam - have shaped cultural beliefs all over the world for thousands of years. The belief that god is outside of us, judging us, loving us and occasionally coming to our aid if we are good is entrenched in our minds as the truth about divinity.

We are not even sure that god exists. According to our new priests, the scientists, everything including us is mechanistic and subject to physical laws. Our only reference to god is through organized religion. After the sexual and emotional abuse we have witnessed, there is little faith in the church.

We continue to question the meaning of life, the purpose for living, the reason for suffering and joy and in the life after death. That savage part

---

[4] Levine, Stephen. *Turning Toward The Mystery.* 2002 Harper Collins Publishers, New York, NY:USA, 10-11.

of our minds, the part that wants to howl in outrage at the unfairness of life, searches for ways to be safe and to know that there will be a tomorrow.

We worry endlessly about our finances, our children, our jobs and our futures because we feel vulnerable and alone. We don't like not knowing how to be safe from pain and death. We feel afraid and helpless of our unknown tomorrows and flee back to the world to immerse ourselves in our lives.

We believe in the worst of ourselves, both individually and collectively. We use the examples of war, famine, overpopulation, pollution and social protests to prove it. When we look back at our known history, we see more of the same.

We are told that we are destroying our planet and we worry that god (or life) will find a way to strike us dead to fix the problem. We talk about Armageddon or the end of the world through war, famine and pestilence, even though we are not great practitioners of faith in God.

Noah's flood[5] and the Holocaust[6] are powerful symbols of how these punishments could happen. In Noah's case, according to the Bible, it was God who got angry with people for not following the correct rituals for worshipping Him. God instructed Noah to build an ark and rescue all the animals in the world while God created a huge flood that was supposed to wipe out everyone except for Noah and his family.

During World War II, the Germans incarcerated many people into concentration camps because they did not fit Hitler's belief of perfection. This was known as the Holocaust. The largest percentage of the camp inmates were Jewish people but the intelligentsia, union leaders, homosexuals and enemies from other countries were also included. Hitler and his army exterminated the people who didn't fit into the Third Reich's idea of the perfect human being.

Many Germans believed in what Hitler stood for. As well, it was frightening for people to speak out against Hitler because they didn't want to be ostracised and killed too. Belonging and the fear of death are powerful needs to humans and we can be manipulated into being mute or apathetic.

The Holocaust is an example of how man's inhumanity to man

---

[5] *Wikipedia.* 2016. Noah's Ark. Last modified January 20, 2017.
[6] *Wikipedia.* 2017. Holocaust. Last modified February 20, 2017.

without god's protection can seem to be brutal, vicious and merciless. The Holocaust helped to spawn the atheistic movement in today's society. After all, we argue, if there really is a god out there, he would have saved us from those horrors or not even have allowed them to occur. Ironically, there are almost as many atheists in the world today as there are Roman Catholic Christians.

We suffer from a strong underlying feeling that we are only pawns prancing across the stage of life, victims of forces in life beyond our control. We hand over authority for our lives to our governments, our schools and our gods but we have no faith in our institutions because of the graft and corruption we see within them.

We also fear that some unspecified or unknown bad-luck god could punish us because we have not honoured all of its rules. We believe that God lives so far away from us, we are not sure of what or who it is. We assume that we cannot attain our goals of peace on earth and good will towards everyone (let alone for ourselves) because of our shortcomings in our relationships with ourselves, other people and the planet. This feels very real and painful to us and we not only worry about the present but about tomorrow, as well, since we cannot control what happens to us.

That is why most religions have rules to be followed. We will be rewarded not only in the present, but will also be protected in the future if we just do what our priest, pastor or religious professional tells us to do. In a great many religions there is a promise of a reward in Heaven for being a good congregant. We eagerly follow our religion's rules so that we can be safe and secure from our unknown tomorrow and our final death.

In our present financial and environmental climates, it appears that the world is falling apart due to humanity's wars, disease, violence, terrorism, hate and greed. Fear stalks us as the known and familiar seems to be threatened by a way of life transitioning into an unknown tomorrow. We don't know if global warming is real or why there is a problem with overpopulation. We are afraid for the next generations. News programs constantly assure us, that indeed, we do need to worry about life, death and tomorrow!

Our uncertainty lies in the fact that we're not sure that we'll be safe in the world without a greater authority to protect us. In fact, we have been trained to look for a greater authority rather than trusting ourselves. We fear life because of the discomforts, pain, endings and death and we don't know or understand that we are the human part of divinity.

It seems, though, that even when we do not believe in god, when times get tough we reach out to something we believe is greater than ourselves. We look up and ask the universe for help.

We ask for forgiveness, salvation, succour and hope based on the belief that somewhere out there, something cares about our lives and who we are. We even blame "Him" and hate "Him" when things go wrong and thank "Him" when things go right.

No wonder discussions about god are so intense. Our relationship *to* god is intense. We very rarely examine our beliefs about who god really is and after failed attempts to negotiate with a god out there, we tend to move on with our lives and ignore god unless socially necessary.

Think about god for a moment. You know, the one we were taught about from watching Christmas shows on television, attending Sunday school or absorbing our cultural understanding of god. How do we relate to that god? Does that god feel close and caring? Is there yearning towards wholeness that is fulfilled by that belief in an outside god? Is there a wanting for more in life? Do we want to know who we are and what our life means as a human being? All of these questions are important because what we believe about god affects our lives. It is difficult to examine our beliefs because that brings us back to the edge of things that go bump in the night and leaves us feeling stranded and alone.

In all of this, we continue to try and learn the rules of behaviour to negotiate safety and a happier life for ourselves with god.

Tomorrow is an unknown part of our lives. We build a story about tomorrow based on yesterday, our beliefs, fears and worries, and then we attempt to appease god.

We pray to god and hope that god will take care of us. We pray for goodness, mercy, money, food and a roof over our heads. We repeat positive affirmations and mantras to ensure that we have a positive future. We also try to be good human beings because we are not in control of our own reality and an outside god is. In our minds, we worry that we haven't negotiated appropriately with all the powers that be and that means anything can happen.

In contrast to our fear for survival, we crave feeling whole and safe from the uncertainty of life and death. We develop cultural and capitalist beliefs of success to give us a sense of security and comfort. We amass money, material possessions and personal relationships but the disquiet persists. We are not so certain that all of those people or possessions will keep us safe in the event that there are parts of life that we cannot control.

Death is frightening because we don't know anything about it. We cannot go beyond living to experience death. Many philosophers and theologians profess that there is life after death and if we follow their way, we will not be afraid of death.

We could believe that death is simply another dimension after life but we don't really know that. We have heard many tales of people who have died and seen a light at the end of a tunnel. We have even heard of people talking to others in that white light. Yet we still are uncertain and fear the ending of our own consciousness.

The Christian message of redemption and life after death is one reason for that religion's popularity. By believing in heaven, people have faith in meeting their maker after death.

Yet, life after death is unknown and the problem is to understand how to make life worth living. If we go to work every day to an unfulfilling job and then go home at night to boredom, fatigue and the television set, we dream of a better tomorrow. Unfortunately, by the time we are retired, tomorrow has been put off for so long that it seems impossible to change life into something different.

When we imagine dying, we become aware of how little we have lived. There is a saying attributed to a man named Bill McKenna: "Life is not a journey to the grave with the intention of arriving safely in a pretty and well-preserved body but rather to skid in broadside, thoroughly used up, totally worn out, and loudly proclaiming WOW- What a Ride!"

Living fully implies being in life. It suggests that we are not here to be safe but to experience the planet as a living, breathing, creative place to be. Otherwise, there would be no point to our dreams.

When we seek safety from the unknown and fearsome tomorrow, we rely on something to protect us, whether it is a god, social status or material possessions. Freedom from the fear of tomorrow is our acceptance of life and our confidence in our right to be here.

What we want to do is sleep at night and know that the boogieman is only a story told to children. Unfortunately, life has bumps and that is what we are afraid of. We may be robbed, raped or hurt emotionally. We may be fired, tortured or belittled. These are some of the boogieman experiences that our minds seek to protect us from.

No matter how we plan for tomorrow, we cannot control it. Freedom is being part of something greater than our separate selves and learning the skills to participate in what happens next.

The purpose of all of our beliefs and storytelling is to control the unknown tomorrow and death. From the time when we are young to the day we die, we are afraid to fully live and to explore our potential because we don't know who we are. Instead, we are taught to conform, to fit in and if necessary to quell any rebellious spirit in the daily order of things. In this way, life goes on. Based on our fears and beliefs, we are taught that we need someone or something to protect us from life.

When we are young, we only think about today. As we get older and experience setbacks in life, we lose trust in our purpose in the world. We give up faith in ourselves because we think that we have failed our goals by not becoming our social icons.

We never thought that the main goal in life is to participate in the experience of living. So here we are: being god, feeling sorry for ourselves and afraid of tomorrow.

If we don't create a tomorrow in our minds, we believe that we will be out of control of our reality. The outside world of strangers and unforeseen events could harm us or devastate us in some way and we believe if we counter the worry with logic and planning, we will be safe. If that were true, there would never be any car accidents, unemployment, theft or other disasters.

Try this exercise for one week: don't think about tomorrow. Obviously, if your child is needed at a sports activity, that has to be planned but for yourself, don't plan. Be involved in everything as it happens. Watch what your mind does, how it works at telling you a story of what is going to happen if you do this or that. Then see what really happens.

Winning the lottery is a great tomorrow story. We believe that if we have a lot of money, we would be free from our inner yearning towards life.

A great tomorrow-worry story could be called "Under the Bridge." It starts like this: Tomorrow I could lose all my money and have nowhere to live because I can't pay the rent. I will have to go and live under a bridge.

While I am under the bridge, people will laugh at me and feel sorry for me and I will be alone. While I am alone, nobody will care for me if I get sick and because I live under a bridge, I won't make it to the hospital.

I will lie under the bridge alone and unloved and when I die, nobody will care.

Isn't this a sad story?

It is one that is practiced daily by many people in one form or another. It is not the truth. It is one of our fears of being unsuccessful and unsafe while living.

Our fear of tomorrow is based on our mind's perception that we will not exist unless we think into the future and take care of it, while being blind to the fact that life is waiting for us right here. This is not about the big things in life like going sky diving or mountain climbing, but the little things: the touch of someone who loves us, watching an eagle fly overhead, seeing trees blowing in the wind and the feel of breath moving in and out of our bodies. We are alive because we are part of creation, the living, breathing gestalt of life.

Meanwhile, we paint ourselves a future with our beliefs and stories and then we react to that future as though it were the truth. We feel let down if the future doesn't go according to our plans and blame ourselves for being failures.

Joanie was a woman who moved to Hollywood to become an actress. She believed she was beautiful and could easily get a job acting based on her appearance. She had no education in acting and no real plan beyond going there and meeting the right person. She had seen many movies based on that theme and it seemed like a good idea for her.

Unfortunately, things did not go as planned. Instead, the first week she was there, she was beaten up and had all her money stolen. Joanie became depressed and suicidal because she felt she was a failure.

She went back home, joined a theatre group as a volunteer and got a job working at a local supermarket. She felt she had fallen very far from grace. One night, in desperation, she screamed and cried out her loneliness and suffering in the emptiness of her apartment. She became so exhausted she could not do anything more than lie on her bed and simply be.

Suddenly, there was a sense of oneness, a feeling of grace and forgiveness and she knew that life wasn't as much about her belief of being successful in her career as it was about who she was as a person. She was a human being and she didn't need to become any more perfect than she already was.

To let go of fearing tomorrow and to trust our right to be here requires great courage because we believe we are powerless. It is a leap of faith in ourselves to believe that we are more than a mechanical body and mind whose only purpose is to live and consume.

Maybe tomorrow will happen or it won't. Uncertainty is our mind's greatest enemy and creates great anxiety and stress. We are insecure with not knowing about how to solve our fears and be safe. We feel that it's our duty to know and protect ourselves from unforeseen threats. Otherwise, we would be stupid in the truest sense of the word.

When we are afraid, our fear stories block out all of our good experiences of life. Until we can understand that our fears are belief driven, we will be a slave to them.

Tomorrow is uncertain. That is a truth, just like death is unknown. Does this mean we have to be afraid?

If we accept that tomorrow does not exist today and we don't know about death, then all of the safeguards we have put into place to protect ourselves make no sense; they are nonsense children's rhymes to create a feeling of safety from death and tomorrow.

No matter how well we plan our future, it doesn't turn out as we thought. We then think, "Ah, if only I could be in the present, then I would be at peace. Tomorrow and yesterday are stories but today is the truth."

Then today becomes a story of yesterday and tomorrow combined into feelings of anxiety as we go about our business. We torment ourselves with the effort of trying unsuccessfully to live in today.

What we really crave is to accept that we are whole and not broken. We want to feel at peace even in the face of grave danger. As we discover ourselves by deciphering our ability to create beliefs and stories, we can experience our lives fully. Then the feelings of powerlessness and fear fade, and trust in who we are occurs even with life's pain and suffering.

When we rely on an outside god that we have to propitiate, there is a level of uncertainty about whether or not god is even listening.

Within our craving for oneness is our seed of self-discovery about who we are. As our beliefs shift to being god, there is faith that we have a role to play in our lives. We are the main character in our one-person play and we can create plays with every other character in the world. Believing in ourselves can develop into an impetus towards self-responsibility, being human and feeling joy.

Imagine experiencing our world as a gestalt of creation and energy that we actively participate in both individually and collectively. We are in the driver's seat. It is our life and our reality. By accepting and being responsible for our perceptions of reality, we can move from being pawns in life to paying attention to who we are.

We have tried our whole lives to please others and fit in with our families, friends, work and society. Imagine instead that we already belong. It is not about fitting in as much as it is about self- acceptance and faith in ourselves that we are part of life.

We have the ability to shift our perception from "us versus them" to "we are all in this together." What is required to overcome our fear of life is to let go of who we believe we are - that we are the pawns in life - rather than the participants.

We are allowed to stop negotiating with an outside god and discover our own voice within. We can trust that whatever happens in life is perfect because we are part of it individually and collectively. It is when we feel connected to all of life that we feel in harmony with living and the yearning for oneness is transformed into love.

Today, we live in the Age of Reason. This began in the 1600's in retaliation against the Catholic Church's control of society. After at least two severe plagues, religious dogmatism was extreme and Europe was dominated by superstition and fear. The Church held power through fear of being burnt at the stake, threatening ostracism and denouncing sin.

In time, countries that were not Catholic challenged traditional thought and scrutinized all beliefs for objectivity. This new philosophy of objectivism was called science and anything you could not use your five senses to know and understand was looked on suspiciously. Objectivism only considered that which was true if it was proven to be outside of a person's biases, ideas, opinions or feelings.

The mantle of intellectual leadership of this new scientific thought fell to René Descartes. He is considered the father of modern philosophy. Descartes said that human souls are united to mechanical bodies. Therefore, memory and learning must be functions of the body and are mechanical rather than of the mind or soul. This is called the Cartesian dualism of body and mind and the scientific distinction of the two remains today. The soul is the realm of religion; the mind is the realm of the psychologist and the body is the realm of science.[7]

What has not been accounted for is our own drive towards the experience of self-transcendence. We want to know that our lives are not in vain. We want to feel a oneness with life, a sense of being, belonging and a knowing that no matter what, we are safe within ourselves.

Our greatest religious leaders and speakers symbolize that yearning. Mahatma Ghandi showed faith in himself with peaceful dissent and won freedom from Britain for India. He also had a great trust in life and in people. Buddha sat and meditated for years until he connected with himself and understood life. Jesus, a teacher of life, love and redemption, said we were no different than who he was, and that all we need is faith that we are children of god.

We want to be like our leaders, but cannot imagine how we can be that spiritually developed. We imagine that spiritual development is something other than who we are. We think that spirituality is something about being perfect and that we can only attain it by chanting "Om," practicing yoga and going to India to work with a guru.

We believe that we would have to turn away from life and its pleasures and we would have to choose a religious or spiritual path to be free from our yearning for oneness. We have been taught for over four thousand years that we need to be more than who we are and that we need someone more connected with god to intercede on our behalf.

As citizens of the Age of Reason, we believe in science but feel there

---

[7] McLellan, J., Dorn, H. (1999) *Science and Technology in World History*, Baltimore, MD, USA: Johns Hopkins University, 246-273

must be more. When we are quiet and still, we feel oneness with life but our cultural beliefs create a block and we have trouble believing we are god because of the religious connotations.

The oldest religion in the world is Hinduism and the oldest branch of it is called Advaita Vedanta.[8] Advaitans believe that we, our true selves, are the same as the highest metaphysical reality, god or Brahman (the absolute consciousness). Their literature says that we can experience Brahman or the Absolute as we gain knowledge of our selves through hearing, seeing and meditation.

In today's scientific world, we yearn towards the *mystery* of life. Stephen Levine says that we also call the *mystery*, the perfect order, with names such as Tao, God or Buddha.[9] He then goes on to explain that as we turn inward and explore ourselves that it is like an unknown journey. First, we investigate the psychological but as we move deeper than our mental constructs and beliefs into our search for something more real, there are levels of understanding that direct us into wholeness.

In all of our material wealth, we still feel a lack of something. Perhaps it is the experience of the absolute or the lack of participation in something greater than our everyday experiences.

If we put aside our beliefs about a religious god and simply accept all of life, our experience could be freeing.

I am deliberately using the term god to help us understand that we belong here. We are not Adam and Eve living on the planet – born and suffering the original sin of defying god. We are god and we can experience this ourselves and discover who we are.

---

[8] *Wikipedia*, 2017. Advaita Vedanta. Last modified February 9, 2017. https://en.wikipedia.org/wiki/Advaita_Vedanta
[9] Levine, Stephen. Turning Toward The Mystery. 2002 Harper Collins Publishers, New York, NY:USA, 10-11

Using the term god is not about worshipping or being in control of an outside force but understanding how our lives are part of the gestalt of being. While it is difficult to shift from a cultural belief of God to a personal experience of being god, it is worth doing because of our desire to be whole and free from worry.

WHAT IS GOD?

According to religious philosophy and scientific thought, the universe was somehow created. Religion says, "god created" or "creationism." Einstein spoke of quantum theories and science explains: "the universe banged into creation and nurtures us with stardust."

Our drive towards a fuller life is experienced globally by people of all faiths. We call the feeling of the divine - God, the Absolute, Christ, Allah, Bodhi, universe, luck, all that is and anything else that helps us to describe our mystical feelings.

For a long time, we have felt there is more to living than this material world. Throughout the ages, religions have developed alongside our civilizations. We have always created god. Our main faiths have included the Vedic and Buddhist understanding that we are part of absolute being, as well as Judaic, Christian and Muslim creeds of a single outside god. Our beliefs have inspired us to higher ideals, given us hope in life and purpose in our daily lives.

It appears that we have always tried to interpret the metaphysical world and it is only in the last six millennia that we have put down any records of what we have thought. Since Sumeria in Mesopotamia, we have written down our beliefs and practices about the mystery of god.

Although our world of today feels like it has been here forever and the thoughts we have of religion feel real - with the perspective of time - we can see that it hasn't mattered what god or gods we believe in but rather how we feel about them. Historically, we have always believed in an afterlife besides the physical and we have understood that there is more to life than struggle, pain and short lives. The experience of being part of god as opposed to being simply earth material is not new.

Our ancestors looked up at the mystery and tried to understand what it all meant.

Seven thousand, five hundred years ago (5500-4500 BCE), Proto-Indo-Europeans,[10] or the prehistoric people of Eurasia, were the first known practitioners of religion. They were mainly polytheistic and worshipped natural gods such as the sun, the moon, the dawn and the storm god. They buried their dead and may have believed in the other world (of the dead) that was guarded by a big dog and the dead got there by crossing a river. They also believed that there was a world tree with fruit that gave immortality and was guarded by a serpent or snake.

The Proto-Indo-European religion provided the roots of other religions in their vicinity. Proto-Indo-Europeans travelled widely around Eurasia and settled in many areas including the Aegean (early Greece), north of Europe, central Asia and southern Siberia. Many of the early Greek and Roman gods were renamed from the gods of the Proto-Indo-Europeans.

Six thousand, five hundred years ago (4500 BCE), the ancient Proto-Semitic people arrived in Mesopotamia, the area between the Tigris and Euphrates Rivers and between the Mediterranean Ocean and the Persian Gulf of today. Sumeria, the southern country of Mesopotamia is often referred to as the cradle of civilization because it was the first place where complex cities developed. These people were mainly of Afro-Asiatic descent according to the early Sumerian texts. They were polytheistic and their major god was a sky god called Anu. Eventually their priests and prophets developed a complex hierarchy of gods and goddesses and a creation story of how the world and mankind came to be.

The Sumerians were just as sophisticated in their written language, social customs, cities, government bureaucracies and religious practices as we are today. The priests ran the temples and the citizens gave daily sacrifices, practiced their trades, educated their young and had their social lives around their temple. They wrote of their religious beliefs, their legal contracts - including real estate - and their trade deals with other cities

---

[10] Wikipedia. 2016. History of Religion. Last modified May 17, 2017. https://en.wikipedia.org/wiki/History_of_religions

and countries. They were a wealthy nation and had influence in the known world.

It was in Mesopotamia that god spoke to Abraham for the first time and told him that if he worshipped God, only God, that God would give Abraham and all his kin the land of Israel. This was the beginning of the Judaic religion, which has survived to the present day.

A thousand years after the rise of Mesopotamia (between 1450 BCE to 1250 BCE) Moses received the Ten Commandments. This contract between god and the Judaic people decreed that they would be monotheistic to their god in return for having their promised land returned to them.

Gautama Buddha was the founder of Buddhism (563-450 BCE). Today, Buddhism is the sixth largest religion in the world. The Diamond Sutra and the Sutra of Hui Neng describe the process of oneness with the divine mind. Buddhists believe that life is an illusion and there is only god.

Two thousand, twenty-two years ago, 4 CE, Jesus, the Christ, (4 CE-33CE) lived and died, leaving a legacy that changed many lives. Christianity is now the largest religion in the world. According to the *New Testament* in the *Bible*, Jesus gave a simple message of love and faith.

Muhammad ibn 'Abdullāh, the founder of Islam (570 – 623 CE), is considered by Muslims to be the last prophet sent by God (Allah). They believe that the *Quran*, which is the religious text of Islam, was revealed to Muhammad by God. The religious, social, and political tenets that Muhammad established in the *Quran* are the foundation of Islam. Muslims believe that there is one God, Allah, and that this oneness is central to their spirituality. Islam is now the second largest religion in the world.

In the nineteenth and twentieth centuries, there began a schism between religion and culture. There was the seed of doubt about whether or not god existed.

Frederich Neitzsche wrote about the death of god in his 1882 collection called *The Gay Science*.

This is what the madman in his story says: "God is dead. God remains dead. And we have killed him. How shall we comfort ourselves, the murderers of all murderers? What was holiest and mightiest of that the world has yet owned has bled to death under our knives: who will wipe this blood off us? What water is there for us to clean ourselves? What festivals of atonement, what sacred games shall we have to invent? Is not the greatness of this deed too great for us?"[11]

Today, Israel and Palestine are at war. There is the rise of Isis and terrorism and a cynicism about god in general. In England, when a poll was taken on religious beliefs, a large majority answered that they were Jedi (from the *Star Wars* movies).

It seems that we have not recovered from Neitzsche's death of god and there is emptiness in our world filled with both society's materialism and our yearning.

We have looked outside of ourselves for the divine for thousands of years. We have worshipped and propitiated many gods in an effort to be safe and secure because we have felt helpless with an apparently whimsical life. We have not been able to control our world or our lives to our satisfaction and our feeling that there must be more, that we need to complete who we are, is still a force in our lives. We have turned away from god in large numbers and instead believe that science can give us the answers we need.

Incredibly enough, science returns us to the mystery.

Mankind has been looking up at the stars for as long as we have been alive. Astronomy or the study of celestial objects such as the sun, the planets, the stars and the moon, originally religious and mythological, are our oldest sciences. Calendars were set based on the observations over the centuries of the sun and the moon, marking the day, the month and the year into mathematical models based on agriculture. The most commonly-used calendar, to this day, is based on the calendar started by Julius Caesar in the year 46 CE. This calendar divided the year into twelve months of alternating thirty and thirty-one days. The Julian calendar was based on 365.25 days in the year, and was originally proposed by the Greek astronomer, Callipus, in the 4th century BCE.

The Ancient Greeks believed the universe was geocentric (all planets

---

[11] Wikipedia, God is Dead. January 25, 2017. Revised July 7, 2017. https://en.wikipedia.org/wiki/God_is_dead

and the sun, rotated around the earth). They developed realistic models of nested planets to understand the stars above them.

Four hundred years before Jesus was born, Aristotle, a Greek philosopher, suggested that the universe was made of concentric spheres whose circulation moved the planets around the earth. He stated the idea that "everything happened for a reason" and viewed the world as naturally occurring phenomena that one could learn to understand instead of being a divine mystery. He was one of the forerunners of scientific thought and has had great influence on the Western world from the Middle Ages to today.

The world as the center of the universe theory lasted until the sixteenth century. The revolutionary idea that the earth and all the planets rotated around the sun was hypothesized by Copernicus in his book, *On the Revolutions of the Heavenly Spheres*, in 1543. This was called the heliocentric universe (everything rotates around the sun) and was the beginning of the Scientific Revolution based on reason and experimentation. He used a telescope to view the night sky and spent many years doing astronomical calculations of the planets, the moon and the sun. Copernicus used mathematics and modelling of the planets to explain their solar revolution. His work was published the day he died and was widely distributed throughout Europe. It caused political and religious upheaval because it challenged the accepted truth that everything rotated around the earth. It was the beginning of understanding how our world fit into the universe.

In 1613, Galileo, a mathematical genius and astronomer, published a book supporting the heliocentric model of the universe. Unfortunately, this was at the height of power for the Inquisition and the Catholic Church charged him with being a heretic. The Church said he contradicted the Bible and Galileo was told to recant in favour of the geocentric model of the universe or be burned at the stake. Needless to say, he recanted in order to save his life.

Galileo was placed under house arrest and lived there until he died. While under house arrest, he wrote a book called *Two New Sciences* proving that kinematics, or the geometry of motion, could predict the velocity, acceleration and motion of all objects due to air resistance and friction affecting the moving object. The proof of the causes of motion on objects paved the way for science to try to unravel the natural laws of how the world behaved.

In 1687, Isaac Newton published his book, *Mathematical Principles of Natural Philosophy*. He proved, beyond a shadow of a doubt, that our planetary system rotates around the sun and that the movement of celestial bodies is governed by the same gravitational rules as the earth.

This was revolutionary, considering only seventy-four years previously, Galileo was threatened by the Catholic Church to recant or die.

For three centuries, this was called *Newtonian physics* in his honour, until it was renamed in the twentieth century. With the advent of atomic and quantum theories, the name was changed to *classical mechanics* and science changed its understanding of what constitutes reality.

When we look at the world, we see the laws of classical mechanics. We understand gravity because things fall. We understand astronomy and how time and space affect celestial objects when we look out into space. We also understand how gases, fluids, projectiles, parts of machinery and time work based on Newton's mathematics and proofs.

Newton's world intuitively feels real to us and it is hard to imagine anything else affecting us. It seems common sense and we feel secure with this everyday reality. We can see the force of nature in the majesty of a sunrise or sunset.

We live with opposing values - good vs evil, light vs dark, Christianity vs Islam and many more opposite values. God as the supreme creator makes sense because we believe all of creation must have all come from somewhere before the Big Bang came into existence. The world, the universe and what our five senses tell us seems so real.

Atomic and quantum theories blow our comfortable, knowable and secure model of reality apart. In our macroscopic world, classical mechanics apply but in the microscopic world, things are very different.

Leucippus, a Greek philosopher from the fifth century BCE, is considered the first person to conceptualize the idea of little primary parts of life making a larger whole. He called these little bits atomos, which means indivisible. His student, Democritus, added to his work and both together created a scientific model of atoms that was based on a mechanistic view of reality. They hypothesized that our material reality broke down into little bits.

In the early nineteenth century, chemists started to use the ancient Greek term, atom, to explain chemical elements. These elements were defined as a material that cannot be broken down or changed into another substance. Elements were thought of as the basic chemical building blocks of matter. John Dalton continued the earlier chemists work and in 1808 published his textbook called *A New System of Chemical Philosophy.*[12] In his book, he used the concept of atoms as being the tiniest bits that made up the unbreakable materials in chemical elements such as tin and water.

He proposed that each chemical element is made up of one type of atom which can combine to form more complex structures. For example, water is composed of two atoms of hydrogen and one of oxygen (H_2O).

It requires 8.36^{1024} molecules of water to make a glass of water, according to *The Naked Scientists*[13] website. When we drink water, does it feel like atomic particles? Or does it just feel like water? There is a subjective challenge between our classical mechanistic world and our understanding of atomic and quantum mechanics.

If we were microscopic, our world could look like this - where all the atoms join together to create things, including us.

....
....
....
....
....

If we lived in this microscopic world, we would laugh at the idea of material things such as people, chairs and trees being reality. Everything is more fluid and changeable in the atomic and quantum worlds.

In 1897, J.J. Thomson discovered that the atom was divisible. He ran electricity through a sealed glass container which held two electrodes separated in a vacuum. Doesn't that sound just like a light bulb? Of course, he got light in the tube. He experimented with the light in an electric field and concluded that the rays were not light but negatively-charged particles which were later named electrons. Electron particles are eighteen times smaller than the hydrogen atom. Hydrogen is the smallest atom in chemistry.

---

[12] Wikipedia, 2016. Atoms. Last modified September 11, 2017. https://en.wikipedia.org/wiki/Atom
[13] *The Naked Scientists. https://www.thenakedscientists.com/articles/interviews/one-theory-rule-them-all. August 24, 2015.*

Ernest Rutherford developed a planetary model of the atom in 1909, where he hypothesized that a cloud of electrons surrounded a small, dense nucleus which was positively charged.

When we look at this model of an atom, we can see a lot of empty space. As a result of this space, scientists questioned why electrons didn't decay and fall into the nucleus and how did the planetary atoms combine to form different elements?

Up to this point, atomic theory was neat and tidy. There were problems with the atoms microscopic sizes and how atoms worked but it was easy to imagine the macroscopic celestial universe being repeated in the microscopic atomic world.

Visualize ourselves made up of carbon, hydrogen, oxygen and nitrogen atoms - tiny galaxies making our bodies. It would look like we are mostly made of air with little dots blinking in and out but somehow, we hold together. We now know that this is done with energy – which creates even more interesting ideas.

We are less solid and have fewer defined boundaries with our surroundings than we imagine, since everything else everywhere is also atomic and looks exactly like these same microscopic galaxies.

Suddenly, our world of classical physics and atomic theory collide and don't make sense. Everything seems so real but is made up of energetic atoms exchanging electrons to create different forms. For instance, the major atomic, molecular components of air are Nitrogen (N_2), Oxygen (O_2), Carbon Dioxide (CO_2), Water (H_2O). We not only are made of atoms, we eat, drink and breathe atoms as well.

Then in the early part of the twentieth century, scientists discovered that the nucleus of the atom was made of even smaller particles. These are called quarks of which so far, six have been discovered. They behave in the weirdest fashion. Sometimes they are particles and sometimes they are waves. It would be like having an apple and apple juice simultaneously. In classical mechanics it can only be apples or juice. It was a mystery how this occurred until Max Planck, Niels Bohr and Albert Einstein came along.

The key to understanding quantum theory was light.

Since the seventeenth century, experiments with light theorized that it was a wave. Think of the sun shining through an aquarium. Now imagine rippling the water. The light ripples too. This experiment was one of two experiments used by Thomas Young in 1803 to demonstrate that light was a wave and not a particle as hypothesized by Isaac Newton. His theory of light waves was accepted as the truth for almost a hundred years until scientists tried to understand what kept the cloud of electrons floating around the nucleus of an atom rather than falling into it.

Max Planck and Albert Einstein postulated that light energy broke up into discrete particles they called photons. Niels Bohr suggested that the energy source that kept electrons from degrading were these photons of light energy. Light, as photon particles, is the energetic driver of electrons jumping from one atom to another, creating various different chemicals. Think about it. We have called ourselves "light beings" and it is the truth. Actually, all atoms everywhere are able to create chemical compositions from the energy of photons. Everything is energized by light.

Through experimentation and physics, it was discovered that subatomic particles and electromagnetic waves (of which light is the energy source) were not simply either particles or waves but contained elements of both. It was also discovered that atoms and molecules can be either particles or waves as well.

What this means is rather than having tiny, little atomic universes with tidy defined electron orbits, electrons use photons to stay in their orbits or jump from one atom to another, based on how many electrons are in the other atom. Electrons are cloudy fields of possibility jumping from their orbits and joining in with other atoms to form our world.

On the microscopic level of waves, particles, atoms, quarks and photons, the macroscopic world of solid objects doesn't make sense. The physical world as seen from quantum mechanics is an illusion.

Thus, reality divides what we can experience with our five senses and what exists but we cannot experience - the building blocks of everything.

Niels Bohr and Werner Heisenberg proposed a theory of quantum mechanics to try and bridge this divide, called the Copenhagen Interpretation. They said that physical systems don't have definite properties until they are measured. The act of measuring affects the physical system, causing the set of probabilities within the subatomic particles to solidify into only one of the possible physical objects immediately after the measurement. In other words, it is the observer effect that creates the solid object. Thus, seeing is believing.

In 1935, Erwin Schrodinger thought the Copenhagen Interpretation of quantum mechanics was ridiculous because it postulated the observer effect onto our macroscopic reality of classical mechanics.

He suggested a thought experiment of a cat in a steel chamber along with a Geiger counter, a small amount of radioactive material and a bottle of hydrocyanic acid. The small amount of radioactive material has an equal probability of decaying or not within an hour. If it decays, the Geiger counter would trigger a small hammer that breaks the flask of hydrocyanic acid which kills the cat. If the radioactive material doesn't decay, the cat continues to live. This is called a superposition of possibilities. The cat is simultaneously alive and dead. The cat is the classical mechanics example of the Copenhagen Interpretation.

According to majority opinion, it is when an observer opens the box that the observer's belief defines whether or not the cat is alive or dead. Niels Bohr, one of the two creators of the Copenhagen interpretation disagreed and said the observer was actually the impersonal Geiger counter, measuring the decay of the radioactive material. Who actually is the impersonal observer? Who decides if the radioactive material is going to decay or not? Who decides luck?

Who decides which baby is created? Who decides who dies and when?

Reality is not as solid as we think it is, nor is it carved in stone. The world we live in is an expression of life creating itself. We experience life day to day and don't pay too much attention to our continual health and physical maintenance.

The Big Bang is science's explanation of how our universe came into existence. The theory is that around fourteen billion years ago, all the matter in the universe was a single point of existence which exploded and continues to expand today. We have no idea what that single point of existence is or was.

Over forty thousand tons of stardust fall to earth each year and have done so since the Big Bang. Some of the dust is as old as the universe itself and some comes from newly exploding stars and galaxies.

Joni Mitchell sang that we are stardust and billion-year old carbon in her song, Woodstock. Stardust, the dust from exploding stars, makes up ninety-seven percent of our bodies. It is composed of carbon, hydrogen, oxygen, nitrogen, phosphorus, sulphur and trace minerals. We would not be here if stars had not exploded billions of years ago to provide the building blocks of life. Nor would we be alive today without the continual renewal of stardust in our bodies. No wonder we look up to the sky for the mystery of life!

We breathe stardust in all day and eat it with our plant and animal food.[14] We are stardust as Joni Mitchell says. As we grow old and die, we return to carbon and become one with the earth again. We become plants and feed animals and get eaten by people. In this way, we are eternal. In our bodies resides the dust of Tyrannosaurus Rex and other dinosaurs and we are the future of the world. We are as old as the universe and are as young as new beginnings. We are a microcosm of all that is self-contained within our bodies. We are stardust, we are carbon and we are immortal.

Life's energy has been called many names. It is the *universal love* of creation, the *chi* of Chinese medicine, the *Tao* of Zen, the *quantum* of physics, the *healing* force of Christianity, the *energy* of Reiki, the *power of healing* in prayer, the *force* in meditation, the power of *affirmations* in New Age and the use of *creative visualization* in mind/body medicine. It is *the aura and chakras* of the body and the sense of *oneness* that we feel when we observe a beautiful sunset. It can be described over and over and discussed under different names. We utilize our energy for health, healing and wholeness and cannot explain how it works.

The scientific name for this mind-body energy is called psychoneuroimmunology or PNI.[15] It unites the mind back to the body two hundred years after Descartes had separated them but brings up more mysteries than it solves.

The mystery began one day in the 1970s when a researcher named Robert Ader was forced to recognise the connection between mind and

---

[14] How 40,000 Tons of Cosmic Dust Falling to Earth Affects You and Me. http://news.nationalgeographic.com/2015/01/150128-big-bang-universe-supernova-astrophysics-health-space-ngbooktalk/ January 28, 20215

[15] Dacher, E. 1991. *PNI-The New Mind/Body Healing Program*. Paragon House. New York, NY: USA

body and how beliefs affect the body in an experiment he was doing with rats. He was doing a conditioned response experiment with the rats. He paired a saccharin-flavoured drink with nausea caused by a drug called cyclophosphamide to create an aversion to the drink. Unfortunately, a problem that occurred over the course of the aversion trials was that some of the rats dropped dead!

Ader hypothesized that there must be a conditioned suppression of the rat's immune system to explain their deaths. At the time, this discovery was startling because science had divided up all the systems of the body into separate fields and believed they were safe from any concept of something as nebulous as mind or god, especially in an animal.

Another of the peculiarities of the mind-body energy influencing the body is the placebo effect. The word *placebo* was derived from the Latin for "I will please" and refers to a physician prescribing for a patient even though he knows the medication has no active ingredients. He pleases the patient by fulfilling his expectation that something will be done. In turn, the patient pleases the doctor by recovering.[16] This effect has been utilized and studied at least since the sixteenth century. Emile Coué, a French apothecary in the 1800s, was so certain that the placebo effect would maximize each remedy's efficiency, that he wrote a small positive note with each prescription.

Today, the placebo effect continues to be examined. Nobody knows why it works. The brain seems to become active and creates the expected recovery in the body. Researchers have found that placebos help the following conditions: pain, depression, acne, anxiety, benign prostatic enlargement, bipolar mania, cough, Crohn's disease, epilepsy, ulcers, headaches, irritable bowel syndrome, multiple sclerosis, arthritis and rheumatic diseases, to name a few.

Psychoneuroimmunology has proven clinically how the placebo effect of the mind/or emotions affects various parts of the body: these include the immune, cardiovascular and hormonal systems. It still doesn't know why it works but proves that we are more than a physical machine.

The term 'energy medicine' has been around since the 1980s. Barbara Brennan, a leader in her field, wrote two books describing a universal energy field. As proof that the field exists, she utilizes the description of

---

[16] Bendetti, F. 2002. *All In The Mind.* Economist, 362 (8261), 83-85

the phantom leaf effect. In this experiment, a leaf was cut and then Kirlian photography was used to show that an aura remained in the field where the leaf had been cut.

She went on to explain how the universal energy field becomes the human energy field or aura. She provides detailed descriptions of auras and chakras and a seven-layer description of the energy field/aura and how it performs different functions. In her book, *Hands of Light*[17], she describes the chakras, or the seven spiritual centers for the body, as transformers that receive and process universal energy.

The idea of chakras (meaning wheel) was written in ancient Hindu and Buddhist texts around 1000 BCE. The energy centers or wheels of light are arranged in a line along the spine. Meditation of the chakras in Tibetan Buddhism is said to heal the split between mind/body and god which facilitates enlightenment or knowledge of all that is. In Hinduism, this is called kundalini. The belief is that there is primal energy coiled in the base of the spine or root chakra and that meditation, yogic practices, breathing exercises and a teacher can help to awaken that energy into enlightenment and bliss[18].

The idea of an energetic field around the body has been written about for centuries. From Mesolithic rituals, to halos around the heads of saints in Christianity and to the psychedelic world of the 1960s, there have been descriptions, pictures, stained glass depictions and meanings attached to these phenomena. Perhaps photons have been observed by seers and mystics for centuries.

Meanwhile, doctors still continue the "sage" tradition of which mysticism and magic are the main – and often the only – ingredient of cure. Knowing this or not, doctors have retained most of these ceremonies due to their clinical usefulness. The specialized knowledge, the esoteric language (Latin), the symbolic stethoscope, the white coat, the aura of mysticism and the aura of emotional distance from everyday life in the

---

[17] Brennan, Barbara A. 1988. Hands of Light. Bantam Books New York, NY USA
[18] Wikipedia. 2006. Kundalini. Last modified June 2017. https://en.wikipedia.org/wiki/Kundalini

modern medical hospital is no different from the early Greek temples of healing. There the white-robed priests went from patient to patient murmuring incantations, laying on healing hands and interpreting dreams and statements made to them by the sick[19] in order for them to be well.

Newton's classical mechanics cannot explain the placebo effect but atomic theory and the Copenhagen Interpretation of the observer effect may be able to. We are not as solid and permanent as we experience with our five senses. Who knew we needed stardust every day to survive? Reality is more malleable than we believed and we are made up of that malleability.

Paul Tillich, a philosopher in the 1950s, wrote that god is being-itself, or the ground of all being. He said that since the time of Plato, there has been this same philosophy, which explains that god is being or all that is. Tillich also described god as the infinite power of being, the ground of being and as the structure of the ground of being[20]. Therefore, god is everything, everywhere and all that is.

Everywhere we look there is a human interpretation of what god is. From Judaism to Jainism, Buddhism, Hinduism, Islam and Christianity, human beings are talking about and interacting with our interpretation of god. All of this is to satisfy our yearning for oneness, self-transcendence and peace. At the heart of each of us, we want to believe that we can be part of something greater than ourselves. Perhaps this is the echo of who we are layered under the beliefs that we have been taught or have learned personally.

We repeatedly speak of our cultural god as something other than us. We go to church on Sundays to worship but during the rest of the week, we get on with our lives without ever thinking about god. We perceive god as being in control of everything except us because we have free will. Yet, when things go wrong, we blame god and pray to "Him" for something better; and when things go right we thank "Him" and pray for more. We believe we will be rewarded for being on the "right" path and feel betrayed when we are not rewarded with what we wish for.

---

[19] Nuland, S. 2001. The Uncertain Art. American Scholar, 70 (3), 123-127
[20] Tillich, Paul. 1951. Systematic Theology, Volume One. University of Chicago Press, Chicago, Illinois

When the Scientific Revolution began five hundred years ago, it created objective-based disciplines that emphasized Newtonian concepts of reality that only included our five senses. To this day, science encompasses our strongest beliefs about the world and its physical reality. We don't question its relevance or truth and simply accept that the world is mechanistic and devoid of the divine in the same way the Catholic Church was never questioned about the reverse.

There are anomalies that still cannot be explained by science. The placebo effect and the mind-body connection are powerful human forces and show how our beliefs can affect our bodies. The ancient theories of energy from acupuncture, chakras and qigong, for example, are still practiced today and there is a concern from people that modern medicine may not deliver as much as it promised. There is still pain, suffering and death in the world, which the priests of science cannot eradicate.

In the dark of night, that three o'clock feeling of despair makes us wish for better and when we are in love, we feel our connection with everything and no longer question our lives. We argue with ourselves and each other for or against the existence of god, but the argument itself belies the fact that *we feel a sense of something within us* when we are at rest, not thinking and simply *feeling part of all that is.*

Our understanding and acceptance of god is about our interpretation of who god is, since it is our beliefs that create our lives.

WE ARE ALL GOD

Based on religious theology, we have been taught that god is far away from us and that we must pray to Him and worship Him in order to receive His benevolence. Yet, since we are part of life, it is more about exploring all the possibilities and experiences that go with being fully alive than it is about being passive supplicants *to* god.

One definition of mysticism is *to become one with God*.[21] Every religion has its mystics who become one with god and speak with god often. They feel a kinship, a oneness and a sense of reverence towards all of life.

All of us are capable of being mystics and having a direct experience of god. Being a mystic is about crossing the physical divide in our minds and accepting being one with god. Enlightenment is the lifting of the illusion of our separateness from god and experiencing the vastness of everything.

We feel wonderful and unafraid when we feel connected to life. Life's creativity is the engine that drives everything. It is the energy that moves electrons to jump from one orbit to another in an atom. It is the energy that creates and blows up stars and it is the energy we use to create our beliefs, our health and our understanding of our place in the world.

We are creative consciousness. We create our lives every day, easily, comfortably and with no effort at all. Imagine how different the world would be if we accepted our ability and created the world accordingly.

We use this creativity daily with our stories of life and our strongly-held beliefs. We would die at times rather than let our creations go. We are the "force," as they say in *Star Wars,* and it resonates throughout our entire being.

---

[21] Wikipedia. 2016 "Mysticism" Last modified January 2017. https://en.wikipedia.org/w/index.php?title=Mysticism&action=history

Tom loved to garden but was afraid of bees. He had no idea of why, but whenever he wanted to garden and a bee came around, he fled. It felt crippling to him to not be able to do what he wanted and he hated himself for that fear.

He tried counselling, acupuncture and positive affirmations to correct his fear but could not get rid of it. One day, sitting in his easy chair, he started daydreaming about bees. He could see himself as a child of around eight years old. He was having a wonderful day by the ocean, playing with rocks and digging holes, when suddenly he looked down and saw that a bee had just stung him on his arm. To him, it had come out of nowhere to hurt him. From that time forward his fear of bees paralyzed him because in his belief, bees stung you out of nowhere for no reason. Suddenly, life was insecure because of bees.

He realized that his fear was from being stung at eight years old and that as an adult he could change that fear. Tom decided to raise bees in his garden and have honey. He set about doing this and learned that bees were wonderful insects and, in time, even stopped wearing his beekeeping suit. He shared his honey with his neighbours, sold some for cash and learned to love his newfound friends.

We are unaware that we creatively project our thoughts about life and that we operate on autopilot rather than manual control. We are just like Tom where we are ruled by our beliefs and fears. We create our world views unconsciously and without volition. We are so mentally busy we don't have time to actually experience what life is doing in the moment. This is not about being here now but about feeling a part of the flow of life all around us. Imagine what we could do if we accepted our divine birthright and learned to swim in that flow. We could shift from our feelings of powerlessness to oneness with life. We could have world peace and abundance with hard work and collective cooperation.

A lot of our values are cultural. We learn to perceive the world based on what we see, hear and understand from those around us. Strongly-held religious or political beliefs can create wars, burnings, torture, hatred, bigotry and discrimination. We believe that our cultural, religious and political beliefs are the truth. Everyone should know that truth, we think. We see those beliefs through our rose-coloured glasses and only question everyone else's beliefs because they are obviously not the truth, since ours are.

Imagine what it must have been like in the Middle Ages to learn that the earth rotated around the sun. Or imagine when Leeuwenhoek looked through his microscope and discovered life. It changed a thousand-year-old practice of medicine to a new science-based one. Our world view is based on beliefs that we accept as truth. When we look at history, ancient beliefs seems simplistic and untrue.

Imagine what it could be like in our future when we travel to distant planets and discover many different forms of life, religions and ways of being!

We are comfortable with our beliefs. We tell ourselves everyday what our truths are and don't see anything else because we only see what we believe is real. Everything else is nonexistent. Imagine how much we don't see or misinterpret every day.

To change our beliefs to understanding life differently is not an intellectual pursuit to be taken lightly. It is gut wrenching and scary to challenge our beliefs about reality. Our beliefs feel so real that when we try something out of the ordinary to see beyond our perceptions, it can feel like we are walking off the edge of a cliff without a parachute.

For instance, try for one day to eat only when you are hungry and stop eating when you are full. Don't watch the clock or use any other visual clues. Discover how hard it is to listen to what you are feeling. Pavlov was right. We are all trained to salivate at certain cues. Now imagine changing that one simple rule of behaviour. Imagine eating only when you are hungry and stopping when you are full, no matter what time it is. It is very difficult to do and it will give you an idea of how programmed we are.

Imagine what it would be like if there were no rules of behaviour. We would have to learn about who we are, what we want to eat, when we want to exercise, where we want to work and who we want to love. Now imagine a room full of people with no rules, all learning about who we are and how we want to be. No wonder we simply follow the rules. It could be chaos if we all decided to wake up at the same time!

Teresa belonged to a religion that was intolerant of those who weren't in her faith. After a while, she found that the intolerance was reprehensible to her and she publicly stood up against it, hoping to change her church. She never believed that her fellow worshippers would kick her out of the congregation and she suffered terribly for about a year after being ostracised. She thought she was going to die of loneliness but slowly she made friends outside of her church and became proud of herself that she had spoken out. She had changed her belief about her life and her life changed.

Another example is with relationships.

Janine complained that her husband and children were always making a mess. She loved a tidy home and resented that they wouldn't keep it tidy. One day, after sitting and resting after straightening out her home one more time, she thought about her family again and imagined how wonderful life would be if there wasn't any family. After contemplating that for a few savoured moments, she realized that her house would be neat and tidy, but she would have no family and that her children and husband were important to her. Her nagging stopped and her family life became happier. When she changed, her family changed and learned to respect how she felt and made an effort to be tidier and continue with being a happy family.

These are just two examples of beliefs and self-hypnosis that we do minute by minute on a daily basis. We run our lives like this, as well as our communities, countries and the world. Nobody is any different. We are all human. We create beliefs and we are willing to die at times instead of looking differently at life.

Learning about ourselves and understanding our own humanity uncovers our oneness with life. Since we are human-creativity beings, think how wonderful the world would be if we could learn exactly how we created our beliefs, challenge what we know and see what happens next.

Imagine a blank landscape where there is nothing: no mountains, lakes, trees, buildings, deserts, nothing. Go ahead and try to imagine it. There is only blankness and suspended feelings. The mind then seeks to fill the blankness with images. It uses our past history, cultural beliefs, fears, hopes and dreams to create an internal image of who we are and what our world is. We then externalize that reality and that is what we perceive as real.

Rather than moving into the mind's story of that blank landscape, imagine instead staying with the blank landscape. Do not try to do anything with it. After a while of staying with the blankness, feelings begin to shift. There is a sense of peace and universality. This awareness can be explored on a conscious level and leads to an experience of self beyond our culture, life experiences and dreams. It is a form of mindfulness. It helps to clear our thoughts and create calmness because we are not caught up in our perpetual stories. As well, it shows the easel on which we paint our life pictures.

Because it is our easel and our lives, we can slow down our internal story and understand how we are in the world and feel a part of life.

We can explore who we are as though we are an unknown entity: throw away our rules about who we are supposed to be, how we are supposed to act, what we are supposed to eat, who we are supposed to love and where we are supposed to live. We have accepted rules all of our lives about who we are supposed to be. Wouldn't it be wonderful to discover that we aren't broken and that we are perfect exactly as we are?

We try to think our way into understanding our consciousness, but our minds are only capable of telling us a story about our beliefs. It is not in the mind that there is self-understanding. Rather it is in the letting go of thinking and allowing the experiencing of ourselves by being self-observant.

Carl Jung, a psychiatrist, a psychoanalyst and a collaborator and correspondent of Freud's, had many dreams of deciphering the human mind. He discovered universal symbols within his patients' dreams that spoke of an unconscious interconnectedness among people. Due to these experiences he became a mystic.[22] He understood that we are all one.

He developed his theory of the collective unconscious to explain the apparent connection of all life and he understood that the "archetype of god" was our inner psychic drive to be fully human.[23] Maslow said the same thing, when he said that we have a need towards self-transcendence. This is as good a term as any for that yearning towards the self-experience of oneness.

Today, there is an increased popularity of the term "spiritual." In the old days, spirituality was connected to religion, but due to the rigidity of the organized church, people have turned away from religious beliefs. Somehow, though, we cannot cast away the need for a greater reality than one that just meets the needs of the physical world. We commonly say that we are spiritual but not religious. In other words, we believe more in the mystical part of life, but not in the god out there who sits in heaven.

Our drive for that mystical connection and security of being has been the main driving force of theology from time immemorial. It has been called many names, religions and philosophies. But it all boils down to that feeling within us that we could be more than this simple, everyday reality.

---

[22] *Jung, Carl G. 1965. "Man And His Symbols." New York: Dell Publishing.*
[23] *Ibid.*

Ironically, we pray to an outside god for help and intervention while we are already that force. There is no spiritual end game or self-improvement where we become better. It is about our decision to understand who we are already that is the game-changer.

We question our being god because we don't always get what we want. The New Age movement subscribed to positive affirmations in order to train our minds to think and manifest what we wanted in the world. We were told that if we wanted something badly enough that it would happen. We read our self-help books and a large number of us felt like failures in our social and economic lives because we couldn't manifest what we wanted. Those of us who were ill and couldn't heal ourselves were told we were failures because we couldn't think positively. Imagine how depressing it would be to feel that it is our fault if we are ill or dying.

It turns out that luck or the holistic everything has something to do with it. We are not in this world alone. We don't function in isolation.

Carl Jung called luck an acausal synchronicity. Jung believed that in a person's life, synchronicity served a role similar to that of dreams. He felt that the purpose of synchronicity was to shift a person's self-centered conscious thinking to one of greater wholeness[24]. Acausal synchronicity is an event that occurs for no reason that we can understand since we don't always have the greater picture of what is going on.

For example, while I am doing my positive affirmations to get a better job, I run into a friend. Through her, I discover that her job (which she just quit) is important as a stepping stone to the life I want. This is acausal synchronicity. This is the right place and the right time event.

Carl Jung believed that his theory of synchronicity explained his concept of archetypes and the collective unconscious. He found that across cultures and age groups, that certain symbols were the same. Freud discovered the same thing when working with dreams and he called it *archaic remnants* because certain dream elements were of primitive myths, rites and ideas. Jung disagreed with this description and said they were related to our instincts and manifested themselves as fantasies and symbolic images. He said that they are without known origin and show up anywhere, anytime in the world. He gave some examples of archetypes such as the wise man

---

[24] *Wikipedia.* 2015. "Synchronicity". Last modified March 25, 2017. https://en.wikipedia.org/wiki/Synchronicity

and the great mother. Still, he said that they are very individual because the interpretation is based on how each person understands them.[25] We are as unique as a snowflake and as whole as a complete blizzard!

He felt that because the archetypes are transpersonal, transtemporal and transcultural, that there is an underlying collective unconscious among all of mankind, throughout the ages. Jung also said that the collective unconscious is different than our personal consciousness. He said the symbols that we experience unconsciously, we use consciously in our everyday lives without understanding where they came from. This has a profound effect on our lives because these symbols aren't something we consciously created and are common to all of mankind.

For instance, one night you dream of a black cat. When you wake up, you wonder if you are in for some bad luck. If you decide to dig deeper in this superstition, you will discover that three thousand years ago, the Egyptians revered black cats as being lucky. Perhaps your dream is telling you to take the risk you are afraid to take. Our dreams, both while we are asleep and when we daydream are full of images that are archetypes that we incorporate into our everyday reality without thought or wonderment. Unconsciously, we function on autopilot.

We are shy of being god and perhaps we like to think that someone else, someone better than us, is in control. We put ourselves into a prison of fear, doubt and shame while waiting for an outside god to help us. We believe it is not up to us to be grown up and responsible for our reality. As we trade our power for safety, we put ourselves into a prison of fear, doubt and shame.

What is safe in the truest sense is that we are god. Each of us can speak to god whenever we want to. Simply look in a mirror and smile. We cannot be emotionally bankrupt. We cannot be free of compassion and brotherhood. These are part of life and so are we. When we search for ourselves outside of ourselves, we get further and further away from this truth as others give us input on *who we should be*. It is difficult to let go of our boundaries and merge into life because we believe that we have limitations. What we really have are blinders to our true selves.

To really grasp this is difficult because it feels sacrilegious or egocentric. Yet the distance between god and us is nonexistent. Try saying it to

[25] Jung, Carl. 1964. *Man and His Symbols.* New York: Bantam, Doubleday Dell Publishing Group.

yourself: "I am part of god" or simply "I am god." Does it feel ridiculous, heavy, responsible or scary?

As we explore life as a human being, we discover that we are not alone but instead we are part of everything. We can feel the grass beneath our feet. We can observe the insects busy in their lives. We can breathe the air and feel great because it fills our lungs without us having to work at it.

A couple of weeks ago I was talking to a man about being god. Bill couldn't say the word god and instead said we were part of the universe. So I asked him why he couldn't say the word god and he said that it just felt weird.

In our world, the 'F' word is more acceptable than the 'G' word because we have consigned god to the realm of religious propaganda as opposed to the realm of living.

Before monotheistic religions ruled the world, there was polytheism or many gods. Each god had its ability and people prayed to it for help. There were household gods, fertility gods, war gods, weather gods, death gods, sun gods and many more. Civilizations such as Egypt, Greece and Rome were polytheistic and many people sincerely believed in the gods of their choice. Mystics were in all those religions so the mystical experience of god is a human one. It is what we feel when we feel our oneness with god.

Science has done a good job of describing a mechanistic universe. This explanation seems so valid that the antiquated idea of an old man who sits up in heaven taking care of us simply doesn't make sense. We turn away from that idea in the same way we grow up and no longer wait for Santa Claus to come on Christmas Eve.

In a group of people I was with last week, one fellow mentioned something about god and he was asked by another fellow if he also believed in Santa Claus. That is how low in repute god has become.

In our mechanistic world there is no god and the only ethical factors we have to consider are our cultural ones. Our myths of wealth, power and sexuality overshadow our compassion for those who do not meet our standards of success. We believe that all people can be healthy, wealthy and wise and it is their laziness and stupidity that holds them back. We even go to war and kill others because we believe that we are better than them.

If we take religion out of god, there is a fullness to life. God is the mystery of being in life that mankind has always dreamed about. Karen Armstrong, in her book *The History of God*, said that her study of religion showed that mankind was deeply spiritual and she suggested that mankind's name Homo sapiens should be changed to Homo religious.[26] We have always had a drive for the divine.

In our mechanistic world, there is no room for god.

[26] Armstrong, Karen. 1993. A History of God. http://www.metaphysicspirit.com/books/A%20History%20of%20God.pdf

Our religious leaders tell us we are broken.

Separating from Our Oneness with God

Babies need love in order to develop properly emotionally and physically. Holding, cuddling and loving babies nourishes their brains and helps them to grow naturally. Researchers discovered in Romanian orphanages[27] that while the children received physical care, they were not loved. As a result, their bodies didn't grow as they should. In fact, for every three months in an institution, they lost one month of growth. The good news was that if the children were adopted before the age of two, their growth returned to normal.

Babies engage their caregivers to love them by being cute, playful and open. If there is no love, they can be prone to high stress levels, lower brain development, severe diseases and infantile death.

Love is intrinsic to human beings. It is a basic drive and need within us. We naturally love and need to be loved. "God is love" is one of the most often-quoted sentiments from the Bible.[28] Paul Tillich says that since god is love and god is everything, then everything is love.[29] In philosophy, *agape* is the word for divine love and is selfless, charitable, non-erotic, brotherly and spiritual.[30]

---

[27] Pappas, Stephanie. 2012. Early Neglect Alters Kids' Brains. Live Science. Accesssed March 11, 2017. http://www.livescience.com/21778-early-neglect-alters-kids-brains.html

[28] The Bible 1 John 4:8 8. Whoever does not love does not know God, because God is love.

[29] Tillich, Paul. 1951. Systematic Theology, Volume 1. University of Chicago Press. Chicago, Illinois. USA

[30] Wikipedia. 2006. Agapism. Last modified November 14, 2016. https://en.wikipedia.org/wiki/Agapism

When we love, we feel whole and complete. The wonder of being in love is that it is not something we have to earn, develop or create. It is as natural to us as breathing. Sadly, we are trained by our failed relationships with our parents, friends or lovers to shield our hearts from love. We do this because personally or socially love makes us vulnerable to pain. When we feel unloved we feel great pain, loss, grief and experience suffering. No wonder we feel so broken! We block the thing we need most in life to thrive because we don't trust love not to hurt us.

When we have a loved one, whether a friend, a lover or a mate we feel part of something greater than us. We feel more than one. There is a saying: "One is the loneliest number." This can be true, or we can go to the source as mystics and experience love itself. That requires trust in life. Trusting life is hard because when we were young we learned to duck from blows in life rather than learning to go with the flow and allow the pain. It is the pain avoidance that creates the blockage of love.

There is another saying that explains life's flow: "Life isn't about waiting for the storm to pass, it is about learning to dance in the rain." These are great words but hard to put into practice because it is scary to trust that we can make it through the pain in life. There are so many things to feel threatened about: loneliness, impoverishment, sickness and death, to name some of our many fears.

We think of children as having the perfect life with no fears or problems. Unfortunately, from the time we are conceived we absorb messages of suffering, pain, fear and separation from those around us. We don't have a chance to maintain or be trained about our sense of self-worth. While authority says to us, "Believe in yourself" they act out, "Pay attention to me because I am right and you are wrong." "What do you mean you don't want to go to bed?" "What do you mean you want to play with those guys?" "What do you mean you don't want to be a doctor?" "Why aren't you perfect?"

As a result of these things being said or implied to us by those who love us, we spend a great deal of our childhood trying to be better because their approval makes us feel loved and healthy. We try to live up to the ideal self created by our authorities, whether they are parents, friends, religion or the government. We don't question if the authority is wrong. There is an inbuilt assumption that we are somehow broken and need improvement.

As small children we experience direct sensations of the world. If something bumps us, we cry. If someone hugs us, we laugh. We don't worry a lot about where our next meal comes from because it is provided for. We are very much in the moment. As we gather experience, we learn that the next meal or next hug might be more difficult to attain than we thought. Our past and our future then glide together to create anxiety about how we are going to survive. This shapes our beliefs about tomorrow.

We add memory to this and we label each experience as good or bad, avoiding the bad and choosing what we believe is the good. As we get even older, we demand of ourselves only good behaviour so that all of our experiences are good ones. We decide that to be mature individuals we have to reach perfection where we are only good people without any bad in us. Bad behaviour is something reserved for the young. Our emotional and social beliefs demand of us not only a material collection of property, both in real estate and with stuff, but a spiritual collection of goodness as well. We want to make sure we have good karma, so that when we die we won't suffer any punishment even into the next life or lives.

Life, with its ups and downs, reinforces that idea. After all, we have been told repeatedly by our parents, peers and religious leaders that we are broken and are not perfect. Many books have been written on the subject of self-esteem but none on the idea that who we think we are is just a story told to us. There is a plethora of self-help books out there on how to fix ourselves to become happy, wealthy and wise. We think that due to the fact that we are somehow broken, we are not attractive, rich or powerful enough to fit in and have social standing. We believe that these qualities are more important than the love and compassion within us for ourselves and all of life.

Also, as part of the illusion of being broken, we feel that we have something intrinsically wrong with us and that when we become better, healed, more enlightened or perfect we can "know" or be one with god. In Christianity, this is symbolized by the concept of the original sin of Adam and Eve's eating the apple from the tree of knowledge. They thought if they knew more or became better they would be more god-like instead of understanding they were already god. After all, we believe that if we are fixed or no longer sinful, then we will be loved, happy and rewarded in life with wealth and success.

When we feel separate and alone, we analyze what is wrong with us and we are advised through our cultural stories that all we need is a Mister or Ms Right. We look outside of ourselves for someone to complete us so that we won't feel so alone. We get part of our sense of being broken from this aloneness. If we were successful, perfect and desirable, we argue to ourselves, we would not feel this loneliness, we would feel whole. Yet when we have a partner, there are still times when we feel intense loneliness and separation. Our sense of separation comes when we don't feel the connection to life. It feels lonely and it hurts, so we fear being alone.

We are not alone. We are not intrinsically flawed and we belong here, so our experience of life can be holistic one. Since we are part of the flowing, moving, creating energy of life, imagine what it would be like to simply experience that, instead of being afraid of what is around the next corner. Life is about "Learning to dance in the rain." Or maybe life is about "Learning to dance *with* the rain."

Our cultural values shape us in ways that we don't think about. Body shape, size, gender and age affect our self-esteem. Yet when we decide to find out who we are, it becomes interesting to learn about being human and how we experience love.

Our minds kick in with their beliefs and scream: "I am here, I worry, I feel, I fret, I have a sense of isolation, I suffer, I grieve and I die." Life definitely feels this way. Yet, as long as we believe our mind's story, we will maunder around in a set of beliefs, feeling separate and alone. Most of the time we aren't even aware that our minds are chattering away to us, telling us all about the reality they have been conditioned to know.

We don't question our minds, our personal selves. Our thoughts feel real. After all, we may question each other's beliefs, but ours are sacrosanct and the truth. The difficulty here is that we don't know how to view our life story and put it into perspective of our life's dreams.

For instance, if we started this sentence: "Since I am god then…" how could we finish that sentence in order to break through the static noise of our stories and achieve our dreams?

We follow explicitly what our stories tell us to do. We believe them; we trust them and we don't consider other alternatives. We tell ourselves stories about the future and then act on our stories as though they were real. The same holds true for our stories about our past. We don't assess our childhood experiences with the eyes of an adult. Our childhood core beliefs about life can be the strongest and most influential of our world-view.

Mary had been abused as a child and she never trusted another man. She learned to distrust men from her experience but her abuse was coloured by her vulnerability, age and sense of powerlessness. Since adults do not have the same vulnerability as a child, relationships could be different at a later age.

Our stories are our reality and they govern our feelings, relationships, economic circumstances and lives. Due to our stories being our truths, it becomes a personal decision as to how we want to separate our fears of life from our perceptions about reality.

In life there is a perceived duality. For instance, there is good versus bad, dark versus light and so on. In the middle, in the space between extremes, is our unknown experience of life. This unknown is the bridge between perceived opposites. Try and become comfortable with the unknown. In the unknown life-experience, middle-space between opposites, we find our answers about who we are.

Do not *try* to provide answers to the unknown to feel secure. Instead, learn about the unknown middle between opposite ideas and values. Imagine it as an unknown country, somewhere to explore and discover. As we relax into the unknown tomorrow, we may discover the bridge is to ourselves.

A good tool for discovering the bridge between opposites is mindfulness. This practice is a conscious and meditative process of bringing our attention to the immediate moment. Originally of Buddhist origin, Jon Kabat-Zinn developed mindfulness as a stress reduction program and uses it in his clinic in Massachusetts. Mindfulness helps to create that bridge between the known and unknown as well as reducing fear and stress. It is a way to know who we are as we watch what our mind is doing in the moment and how it creates the stories of our lives[31].

Mindfulness is something very easy to practice. It is a simple daily practice of watching your mind and how it thinks. It is not a meditation or an attempt to be calm. It is about focusing in the moment.

Try this mindfulness exercise. Find a comfortable place to sit for about half an hour. Focus in the present moment and relax into it. Listen to sounds and other sensory inputs. If any thoughts, judgments about the thoughts or ideas occur, simply allow them to roll by and come back to the present moment. Sounds easy, doesn't it? As you return to the present

[31] Mindful. Getting Started with Mindfulness http://www.mindful.org/meditation/mindfulness-getting-started/

moment over and over again, be present in it. Be aware of the thoughts but don't hang on to them. As soon as you catch yourself meandering away from the present moment, come on back. Stay with the daily practice and in time you will notice being able to stay in the moment longer and experiencing greater relaxation and comfort.

We aren't aware of how we think. The thoughts go so fast and we respond so quickly with our stories to those thoughts, that it requires practice and concentration to follow ourselves down the rabbit hole. As we peel away the layers of our beliefs about being broken, our innate love, our self-love, will begin to shine and encourage us to be more of who we are.

We cannot change our habits of thought by deciding to think differently. They are changed by understanding how we think and create our stories and beliefs. Many times when we look at our stories, we ask ourselves why we think that way. Why do we believe what we believe? Ironically, asking why simply brings up more stories. "Why?" asks us to look for a reason for how we feel. We can find lots of reasons: it was because of my mother, sister, husband, neighbour, or widow down the street.

When we ask how we create our beliefs, we look at the nuts and bolts of how a belief functions. For example, body size plays a very important role in our culture. The average height for women is five feet, three inches and for men, it is five feet, ten inches. Therefore, anyone outside of those averages is either too short or too tall. This plays out with buying clothes, furniture, cars and any other product where body size is defined. If the stuff doesn't fit correctly we take the blame. Another example is right-handed versus left-handed. A left-handed person is constantly adjusting to a right-handed world. If we do not fit into the average, we feel not quite up to the mark. We can develop a belief that we are not good enough and can even spend thousands of dollars trying to shape our bodies to fit in.

Another way we create beliefs is through trauma. This can occur when parents split up and their children feel it is their fault. Somehow, they aren't lovable enough to keep the family together. In reality, it has nothing to do with the children but all the explaining in the world cannot remove the belief. It requires age and experience to understand human frailty.

Being alive is not a Pollyanna-type of experience. There are floods, famine and people dying all the time. That is why we want to know the future. We want to be safe. Being safe is the reason for our stories but when we truly understand that we are not alone, then not one life is ever lost. They are with the whole as we are, in our memories, in the stardust and in the energy of life.

For the thousands of years that we have been burying our dead, we have believed that there is an afterlife. We have given our loved ones tools, food, pets, clothes and poems to take with them to the other world, whether it is Hades, Heaven, reincarnation or something completely unknown. We don't know for sure where we go because nobody has recently returned to tell us about what happens after death.

Since we have no idea what happens after death, in spite of what religions or our beliefs tell us, it makes sense that we understand as much as we can about who we are and how we live while we are alive. Do we really want to live in a prison of fear and suffering? Or do we want to stretch our wings at creation and learn how to fly? As we learn about ourselves, we feel that we are part of something greater than being a single "I" functioning in a mechanical world.

In Aristotle's time, the soul was considered the animating or vital part of humans. The soul furnished people with the ability to live, reproduce and function. The Christian religion says that it is the divine and immortal part of us. The online dictionary defines it as the spirit or essence of a person usually thought to consist of one's thoughts and personality.[32]

When we take religion out of life, god is the animator. Therefore, there is no soul. There is only god.

We work hard to maintain the fractures and fears about life with our stories and beliefs. They maintain the fear of tomorrow and death. We repeat our fear stories endlessly like a program running in the background. We aren't aware that our fear stories repeatedly play because we do our best to ignore our fears and get on with living. It's like trying to not think of pink elephants. The harder we try to not think about pink elephants, the more we do.

Most of the time people try to counter fear stories with logic. Fear is not logical. Our minds use fear to keep us safe from harm. We then try to use our same mind to not be afraid. We certainly aren't aware that security in the world is a mental delusion and that fear of the lack of security is the same mental delusion that maintains the feeling of being broken. Beliefs are very powerful creations.

---

[32] http://www.yourdictionary.com/soul#DYy0Wqjp9GTRHjFO.99

Since we have the perception of separation from god and each other we wait to see what unfolds believing that the god, *out there*, is in control and will tell us what to do or better still, do it for us, like a kind parent. No wonder we don't feel whole; we make god into an image of our darkest selves with all of our sound and fury. It would have to be a pretty stupid deity who thinks that we are good, since we are so full of sin, we believe.

We don't know how to let go of our hard luck stories in order to be at peace with life. We don't understand that the life stories we prize so much are what keep us feeling fractured.

If we are in control and are not god, then our stories are true and validate our reality. We call this free will and a separation from god, created by god in order for us to know god. Talk about convoluted thinking. We believe that if we think loving and positive thoughts and do good works that we will develop good karma. We believe that we will be rewarded for our good behaviour by whatever name we call our separated deity. We don't understand that love and karma are the same thing. Since god is love, we are love and we don't need to gather good karma in order to experience it.

In our self-hatred we feel separate from each other, different and alone. We are untouchable, closed in and suffering. We look at others and somehow they seem happy, together, whole, complete and content. We ask ourselves what is wrong with us and where we went wrong.

We are not alone and closed in. We are part of everything and it is our self-hatred that creates the block between us and being god.

What actually is self-hatred? It is an intense dislike for ourselves. It could be because of the colour of our skin. It could be because we don't like our gender. We could be the wrong size: too short, too tall, too thin, too ugly, too poor, too little or too big. Our dislike is a continual drone in the back of our minds that makes us suffer personally and socially.

Yet who said our social and personal rules are true? Imagine for a minute that every rule we know as the truth, is not the truth. Imagine that everything we have been led to believe about who we are and what we stand for is not the truth but common beliefs.

If we look at our rules of behaviour, none of them are real. Some can be useful. It makes sense hygienically to use a toilet rather than empty our slops in the streets as we did in the Middle Ages. It makes sense to learn to read and write so that we can communicate our stories with each other.

Social rules of behaviour make sense so that there is law and order. In other words, we agree to certain rules for the greater good.

The rules that hurt us are the ones that make us dislike who we are. These rules are the ones that make us feel like failures or not worthy of respect. Some of these are financial rules. Why do we think that rich people are better than us? Why do we think the colour of a person's skin matters? Why do we think that where we live on the planet makes us better than where someone else lives? When we die, all of our bones look the same, regardless of wealth, circumstance or position in life.

Being human makes us equal to each other. We cannot be less than or more than human. What then does being a human mean? We are a branch of a tribe called Homini. We are the survivors of the great apes who learned to walk upright, have highly complex brains, use sophisticated tools and have high manual dexterity.

We have the ability to imagine and create philosophies and stories about life because we are dreamers. We dream of better lives for ourselves and our children. We dream of outer space. We dream of beautiful works of art, literature and mathematics. We dream of justice, truth, a better society and we dream of god.

From the first time we looked up at the stars we felt reverence towards everything around us. We felt the warmth of the sun and the rain as it fell. We saw wondrous beasts and great landscapes and we felt transcendence and called it god. All of life felt so large and we felt so small within its immensity, we wanted the comfort of knowing that we weren't alone in a savage world.

Self-transcendence is a sense of being one with all of life. It is a feeling of being part of the universe and moves us beyond our sense of self to a sense of being one. Self-transcendence is being able to move beyond our world experience to understand that we belong here, have a right to be here and we don't have to change ourselves in order to experience our transcendence. It is our birthright.

The world is still immense and we still feel alone in our suffering. Yet mankind has lived fully on this planet for millennia. We are stardust, we are earthlings and we are self-transcendent.

We love our mystical experiences of god and we don't comprehend that our mysticism exists because of who we are.

BEING HUMAN

I magine yourself in an infinite candy store. Any candy you desire is in that store plus some you don't even know about. The problem is that you believe that only the lollipops are real.

Remember that time when you couldn't find your car keys? You looked everywhere. Yet when you gave yourself a mental rest, you went back and found those keys in the same place you looked in your original search. Initially, the keys were literally not there!

The same is true in our everyday living. If we don't believe in it, it doesn't exist. For instance, if we don't believe in tables, we would walk right by them and not see them. Perhaps if we bumped one, we would wonder what we tripped on.

Our minds are like that. Believing in something really is seeing it. This is called perception. We only perceive what we believe in. It is not about creating reality but about changing our beliefs about reality that can open the blocked doors in our lives.

Human beings, by our very nature, are social creatures. We want to fit in. We have role models within our group or culture and we emulate them and please those we love. As children, we want our parents to love us and we try to behave well so we won't be punished. We carry that model of authority into adulthood and we try to shape ourselves to fit in with the rules of behaviour of whatever society we live in.

We work hard at our jobs, in our relationships and at life. We imagine that if we could feel whole rather than broken, then everything would be perfect and we could get on with our lives. Usually we think something like: "What is wrong with me? If I can fix what is wrong, then I can be loved or I can love" (or whatever fits into our definition of happiness).

The difficulty in accepting our humanity is that we keep trying to become better or more human than we are. The hardest thing there is to do is to have a life without judging ourselves and without trying to fix what we perceive as wrong with us. Instead, we can choose to love ourselves with grace and compassion. Ironically, this is exactly what we want from other people.

It is amazing that when we actually stop and listen to our self-criticisms, how hurtful we are to ourselves. It would be a wonderful change to hear our inner voices saying how great we are exactly as we are right now.

In our culture we speak about people evolving into something better, something more human. When we say we are evolving, what are we evolving into? Can there be super-human? Wasn't that the problem of the Nazis trying to create a super-human race? Also, in order to create something super-human, there needs to be a sub-human to compare to. Again the Nazis spring to mind.

Instead, because of our humanity, we can move away from isolated self-hatred to shared responsibility, love and compassion. That is not becoming something better than we are. It is who we are already.

As part of our life experience, we hate, rage and want. It is almost as though we are culturally encouraged to be this way. After all, if we were happy and confident about ourselves, would we need to be consumers of self-repair and self-development? If we could accept those angry, painful parts of us, we could develop compassion for our pain and learn to let go of the suffering with grace. In that way, we could also extend compassion for each other's suffering and create peace as opposed to hatred.

A good way to understand how we hate, rage and want is to imagine a young child version of ourselves when we first experienced those emotions. *There are actually parts of ourselves that still experience our childhood pain.* We then imagine our adult selves hugging our young child part of us and simply feeling love and compassion towards the young child. By feeling love and compassion for our younger self and accepting those parts of ourselves, we create our own self-peace. This is called inner child work and it useful for self-acceptance. Imagine how that young child could feel if she was raised with the experience of her own self-love!

We judge what is good or bad in the world based on our perceptions of our experiences and cultures. We are comfortable when we feel in control of our goodness and badness. When we have too much perceived bad, we feel broken and in need of repair.

For example, we consider being larger physically a bad trait. A person who is overweight can be judged as lazy, selfish and self-destructive. When we believe that we are overweight, we hate how we look. We tell ourselves that we need more will power to lose weight. We can even be so embarrassed that we don't go out and socialize or join in any community events. We get locked into loneliness and self-hatred and we never question if weight as an issue is even real. After all, body size is culturally subjective.

This is also what our species does globally. We created the United Nations to repair the world based on our concepts of peace and love and we have wars in the Middle East based on our prejudices and competing beliefs. Yet, we are all human beings, living our lives.

Our minds work constantly and unceasingly to give us results, solve problems and create solutions. Our biggest problems are who we are and what we want. It constantly stymies us that we cannot create happy, safe solutions for ourselves, even when we don't know what makes us truly happy.

We want what we lack. We don't want to be poor; we want to be rich. We don't want to be sick; we want to be well. We don't want war; we want peace. Ironically, all the things we don't want, we have. It's as though all we have to do is decide that we don't want something and bam! We have it. That is because we only focus on what we believe is real and we don't see what else is there. We are back to the experience in the candy store where only the lollipops are real.

We experience ourselves as a person, separate and alone in the world. We worry about our lives, careers and purpose in life. We live, love, laugh and are happy, sad and hopeful. We suffer pain, sorrow and deep felt grief at loss. This all adds up to being as human as we are capable of while living full lives. We think that there must be more because it feels like not enough: we need more human, more compassion, more kindness, more awareness and togetherness, more of everything, in order to not feel broken.

No wonder we have trouble with abundance. We believe that we experience more suffering than joy. When we look at our reality, it appears that we certainly know how to suffer more than being joyful. We worry about our health, our finances, our social status, our stuff, our kids, our parents, our governments, our insurance and our lives. Yet, when we look at our lives objectively, we have periods of great joy and happiness. We love our children, our partners, our groups and our communities.

As life goes on and we mature, we ask for a greater understanding of the world as we struggle with everyday questions of survival. Does it ever end? Will we ever find happiness? Will we ever find security? What will happen in the world? Will there always be poverty? How do we find love?

It seems that the pain of life is continual and almost unending. There is great sadness, loneliness and misery. As we look back to when we were kids and how we were cheerful for the most part, it raises the question of when did we give up joy for suffering?

We, as selves, think inside a box called life and culture. We feel safe inside the box and seek success within its realm, even when we feel bad. We learn to maintain the rules of this box and we believe that if we play the rules right, we will be rewarded with social and material benefits. It is difficult to think outside of this box because it is known and it feels safe and real.

The box is a symbol of our personal reality and thought. When we believe that there is an eternal reward or fulfillment for following our personal, cultural or religious rules, it is difficult to go outside that box and pay attention to how we create our lives.

Let us return to the example of the lollipops in the candy store. Imagine one day something occurred that created an opening of our awareness in the candy store and for a minute we saw the whole store in all of its splendour. We knew, without a doubt, that we could choose whichever candy we wanted. We would feel excited, overwhelmed, giddy and then thoughtful of which candy we would choose. These are our dreams.

We imagine or daydream and then we project this into life to make the dreams real. We dream of becoming astronauts and going to distant planets and the universe resonates with the wanting. *Star Trek* is born and we begin to explore space. The drives and dreams of mankind create the future, even about space. When we block this process for safety and we don't believe in ourselves, it creates a sense of frustration and being broken.

On the canvas of life, we tell stories of what is and what appears to be. We discuss in detail our findings and we try to add to our history a sense of wholeness so that we can feel complete with life. When we meet others, we recite our histories to each other and compare our wounds and our tributes. We acknowledge each other's pain and joy. In this way, we form bonds of friendship or competition depending on how we see each other's stories. How often do we actually see the other person for who they are - another human being behaving in a human fashion?

What creates a sense of wholeness? It could be an urge to go climb another mountain or a desire to find out what is around the corner. It is a desire for life that holds us and keeps our passions going, a love of life that is unquenchable. It is when we are in our passion and wonder that we feel great. We are full of energy and life and we feel good, whole and going for it. When we are stuck, afraid, feeling alone and sorry for ourselves, life feels empty and unfulfilled. Yet, it is all life, both the unquenchable and the emptiness.

It seems that the human race feels incomplete when it is not immersed in the doings of life. We yearn for peace and pray for excitement.

For one day, imagine that you are perfectly human and don't work at being anything except who you are. If you believe that you are a terrible person and you hate yourself for being terrible, explore that feeling as perfect in the moment. Ask yourself what terrible is. Experience the emotion of terrible! Don't listen to the story of being terrible. This is not about the story but about the feeling. Understand the feeling fully and let it lead you to the discovery of your humanity. If you feel great, explore that. Feel that emotion in your body. Where is it? Don't ask what created the emotion – simply enjoy it. Being human is a wonderful event. After all, we are only here in this lifetime once. The only way we can learn who we are, is to explore how we function and think. As we understand our perceptions, fear, love, hate, sadness, joy and all other feelings, our beliefs start to shift and there is a greater ease in our lives. We feel more comfortable being in our own skin and those competitive feelings of jealousy and insecurity fade.

When we have an acceptance of ourselves without rationalization or mental storytelling, there is an inner peace that halts our demons. It is the story of the alcoholic whom nobody can help until he accepts his own addiction. Without that self - acceptance, there will be no peace.

The strength to let go of our persona (created by our life stories) can come from hitting rock bottom, the place where it is the dark night of the soul. When we hit this place, all illusions, hopes and fears are destroyed. It feels like hell has opened us up and swallowed us whole. There is no worse emotional place than this. It feels like we are going mad, falling apart and cannot survive. We feel like we are going to die or at least wish that would happen.

At this point, we either go on drugs, alcohol or religion, or we give up the fight for ourselves and surrender to life. When we surrender, either by kicking and screaming our way there, through meditation or whatever, then something beautiful happens: we connect fully and completely with a sense of grace, a sense of perfection and peace that we never knew existed. Then and only then do we start the real work of our creation, which is to explore who we are and thus god itself.

If this sounds esoteric, I am working very hard to not make it so. This is not a spiritual journey to be taken intellectually. This is a gut-wrenching, terrifying experience of letting go of who we believe we are.

Learning who we are is like any other relationship we develop. In order to make it work, it requires absolute commitment to a relationship with ourselves. It requires learning to trust in life since we are engaged in life all the time. Learning to trust life is like learning to trust a best friend, partner or mate. After we love them and get to know them, we accept who they are and overcome our fear of being hurt. Imagine how much harder it is for us to learn to trust life itself since we have no idea what life will bring to us tomorrow. Life for each person is experienced differently. We have different purposes, meanings and goals in life but the feeling of being alive and excited about living is what makes life worthwhile.

Our beliefs are very difficult to break because they define who we are and to give them up makes us feel vulnerable to life. Usually we create new beliefs to counter old ones. It is harder to let go of beliefs and only replace them with our self-knowledge.

A belief is something we think is true, even if there are no facts to back it up.

Let's think about this. A belief is formed based on our personal history, culture and ideology. For instance, I am a female, raised in Canada and my parents had a nasty divorce when I was young. As a female, I have learned to behave in certain ways so that I won't be condemned as a slut or be raped. As a Canadian, I am bilingual, believe in equal rights, social programs and feel loyalty towards my country. Ideologically I believe that socialism can help the distribution of wealth and that nobody wants to be poor.

Who am I? Am I my beliefs? Are my beliefs my creations? Are they real? If I am not my beliefs then what is my real nature? My gender really has nothing to do with who I am. Neither does being a Canadian or believing in socialism.

Descartes said his famous, "I think therefore I am" in an effort to try and define human nature. Is thinking real? Is thinking who I am? When I am watching a beautiful sunset, smiling at a newborn baby or when I am deeply absorbed in a project, who am I?

Nisargadatta Maharaj asked that same kind of questions in 1937 when he went to see his guru, Siddharameshwar Maharaj in India. His guru told him that he had to go back to his pure state before he had his beliefs about "this" or "that" and that he was divine and to trust that was the absolute truth. He was told that his joy and suffering were divine and that he was god and that his will alone was done. Nisargadatta was told to focus on the mantra "I Am" and to stay with that in order to discover his true being.[33]

In his book, *I Am That*, Nisargadatta says that the seeker is someone who is in search of himself and to give up all questions except "Who Am I?" He goes on to say that in our self–discovery we will find out who we are not and that the only thing we can be sure of is that we are. He said that as we go through our thoughts, body, feelings, time, space and beliefs there will be nothing that we can perceive as ourselves. In fact, if we can perceive ourselves, that is only the illusion of perception. He said the more we understand the "Who Am I" the quicker we will end our search and realise that we are the limitless being.[34]

Our beliefs are our creations. We defend them as the truth and can even be prepared to die for them. Wouldn't it be easier to understand our beliefs and to challenge whether or not they are the truth? Do our beliefs hold up to "I Am"?

[33] Wikipedia. 2016.Nisargadatta Maharaj. Last modified March 6, 2017. https://en.wikipedia.org/wiki/Nisargadatta_Maharaj
[34] Douwe Tiemersma, 1981. "I AM THAT". June 1981. Douwe Tiemersma, Erasmus Universiteit, Rotterdam, Holland. http://www.anandavala.info/miscl/I_Am_That.pdf

We are not broken. We are exactly who we are meant to be – Human.

BEING A HUMAN I OF GOD

In our culture we believe in personal happiness and success to help balance the fear of tomorrow and death. We have fairy tale stories such as Cinderella, who started out as an abused stepsister and then with the help of her fairy godmother, married Prince Charming. Abraham Lincoln was an American who represented the same ideal. He grew up in a rustic cabin and taught himself to read and write. He believed in himself so strongly that he became president of the United States of America. Barack Obama did much the same thing in 2008 when he became the first black president of the USA.

We look at those examples and we want to be like them. We want to be heroes and presidents.

We imagine ourselves having a fairy godmother and search for our personal Prince Charming.

By understanding our personal dreams and drives and by having faith that we are more than separate human beings, we could be open to all of life. When we think of our potential, what is it that keeps us underperforming? Perhaps it is our fear of failure or that we have been taught to tuck ourselves in like a turtle and not to make waves. When we challenge ourselves to discover our strengths and follow our dreams, it isn't just about our career, life's path or one's true love. It is about being proud to be a human being and to explore our part in life and understand what that really means.

To explore our consciousness requires great trust. It means being willing to get to know and accept ourselves without changing to become a better person or to be enlightened. It requires the same emotional strength to look at others with objectivity and see who they are without having to change them. It is in that acceptance of self and others, in that holding still of shape-shifting that we discover the deep wellspring within of our acceptance of life, our natural inner strength and our human divinity.

Think about our lives. There are times when things are out of control and we think that we have to fix ourselves to make things right. Then things go well for a while and we congratulate ourselves on what a great self-repair job we have done. We go on diets to lose weight and discover we are no happier. We go to the gym and push weights and discover we are no happier.

We go to counsellors to get the weight off our shoulders and discover we are no happier and then we give up and decide that there is no such thing as happiness and simply wish to reduce our suffering. We believe that by giving up on our dreams, we will find peace. Yet, at the end of the day, we face ourselves in the mirror and wish for more.

In actual fact, we are not broken and there is no need to fix anything. What needs to be fixed is our idea of who we are. We cannot be the perfect ideal no matter how hard we try so we believe there is something intrinsically wrong with us. We never question for a moment about our ideal cultural values. We still have the childhood trust that authority is correct, so if we don't fit in, then we are wrong.

Let's look at some of those cultural values that we simply accept. Money is good - the more the better. People with money must know more or be better than us. If you are not blonde – you are not attractive. If you are not muscular – you are not attractive. If you don't own your own home – you are not a winner. Here are some more beliefs: God is dead or at least asleep at the wheel. Being a conservative or a liberal defines you. Never go outside with wet hair. Apples are good for you and French fries are not. The list goes on. Who said these beliefs were real? What really is the truth about who we are?

I had a wonderful friend who was compassionate and caring towards others but knew beyond a shadow of a doubt that she was a lazy, fat pig. My friend was five feet seven inches tall and weighed sixty-eight pounds. She spent each day in tremendous suffering, wishing she could die, because she felt she was so broken, so unable to be human. Eventually she got her wish and she starved to death.

The story of our beliefs trumping who we are is a human story. It is not confined to this culture but to the human race. For instance, in cultures that believe in reincarnation, some people focus on doing very well in this lifetime so they don't have to return. In Christian cultures, we focus on going to heaven rather than hell when we die, so we won't go to that fiery place. For those who don't believe in a god, there are plenty of material gods available while we are alive: money, power, sex, greed and self-interest. Our stories and beliefs cloud our true selves.

We believe that without self-control, we would end up in anarchy. We would kill each other or have sex in the streets. There is, after all, still war, rape and greed in the world, let alone loneliness, desolation and despair.

How do we break out of the story and be ourselves? It is difficult because the tools we are given in our society start with the implicit idea that somehow we are broken. If this is so, how do we know when we are fixed?

We are love, warmth, connection, oneness, wholeness and happiness. We are the end of the rainbow and the source of contentment. We don't have to evolve to have these feelings for ourselves or from anyone else. When we love another, it is our love that we are feeling and sharing. It is ours simply because we exist, we are born. This is not a gift. Our self-love is our right and our humanity.

In Victor Hugo's story, *The Hunchback of Notre Dame*, a twisted and deformed hunchback, Quasimodo, lives in the Notre Dame Cathedral with his guardian, Archdeacon Frollo. Frollo has a lecherous interest in a beautiful, kind, young, gypsy woman, Esmerelda.

Frollo orders Quasimodo to kidnap Esmerelda and bring her back to the cathedral so Frollo can have his way with her. As Quasimodo is dragging her back to Frollo, she is rescued by a captain of the guard, Phoebus. Frollo frames Quasimodo for the kidnapping and he is beaten and put into stocks. He gets thirsty and begs for water. Esmerelda feels compassion for Quasimodo and gives him some water to drink. Due to her kindness, he falls in love with her.

Frollo is angry with Esmerelda for turning him down for Phoebus and he attempts to kill Phoebus and fails. He frames Esmerelda for the attempted murder because of his jealousy and she is sentenced to be hung. On the day of her hanging, Frollo laughs at her for turning away his sexual advances and in anger, Quasimodo throws him off the heights of the Notre Dame Cathedral.

Emotionally bereaved, Quasimodo goes to the graveyard where Esmerelda is buried and stays by her graveside until he dies eighteen months later.

This is a sad story and it has all the human sound and fury that occur in life.

The name Quasimodo has become synonymous for someone who has a courageous heart but an ugly and gruesome exterior. As he found his heart and discovered his humanity, his exterior became unimportant and his suffering ended.

Close your eyes for a minute and feel how life creates you and your surroundings. Feel your breath moving in and out of your lungs. We don't even pay attention to the fact that we breathe in and out at least twelve to twenty times per minute. We only feel it if the air is acrid or scarce. Imagine if it wasn't automatic and we had to remember. That would be awful. The same is true of our eyes blinking, our heart beating and our senses seeing, hearing, smelling, touching and tasting.

With training it is possible to control heart rate, breathing and the five senses. We are not passive in life. We are an equal opportunity participant.

Wanda was a woman with high blood pressure. it was so high she was in danger of having a stroke. Her high blood pressure had developed over time. She worked a stressful job, ate on the run, and had insomnia. Hers was not a great lifestyle. The only thing Wanda could control, at the time, was her mind.

She went to see a clinical hypnotherapist and learned self-hypnosis where she actually visualized her blood pressure going down to normal on a sphygmomanometer (blood pressure machine).

She learned to listen to what she was thinking about and do relaxation exercises. Three months later, Wanda's blood pressure was close to normal. She was cheerful and optimistic about life and loved her job because she could diffuse other people's stress at work.

If we were mechanical, living bodies that followed only scientific reality, hypnotherapy would not work.

As we do that, we feel a sense of being broken and the cycle of pain repeats itself. We try to fix ourselves by finding someone else to love in order to heal our hearts. If only we could just stay with our love and understand that it is not "from" someone as much as it is us opening our love "to" someone else. The love is never lost. The hurt comes from trying to shut off the love.

I remember a young man, David, who used to clean our yard every summer. He would do odd jobs whenever we required them and over the years we grew to love him. After we knew David for fifteen years, he developed depression and he told us how much he hated us and he walked away from our lives. Our loss was devastating.

At first, I was angry and then I decided to continue to love him. I felt that I didn't want to shut my feelings off about him. I visualized his face and allowed my love. My anger disappeared and I continue to love him to this day. We never saw him again and I miss him but I will always remember him with love instead of pain.

It is our perception of not being perfect that creates our difficulty with living. We can shift that perception by trusting that we are being perfectly human. That does not mean that it is okay to be cruel to others. What it means is we don't hide the cruel part from ourselves. We live with it, learn about it. Discover the characteristics that make up our particular model of a human self. We learn what creates cruelty within humans. We learn to understand with compassion the pain that cruelty creates for other people.

We can explore our suffering to discover our humanity and to understand how we function. Life is our gift to explore and understand even though it is hard to believe when we are in pain.

It is in the acceptance of self that there is peace with self. Imagine for a minute that there is nothing left to fix. We have everything we want and need. We have all the money we want. We have perfect health. There is no war, greed, hate or pollution. Now what? What are we going to do or be now? Imagine that. Nothing left to fix. Who are we and what are we doing? That is our big dream. It is our potential we are looking at. Why not take the risk and be the dream? This is not about a career. This is about who we potentially are.

We experience hate and fear in our lives and we believe that this is wrong. It is not wrong. We are simply a world of people who believe we are not responsible for our own hate and fear and don't know how to have compassion for ourselves. The compassion starts with "I am" and then we can open to being self-responsible.

If you are mad at your spouse, then that is what you are. There is nothing wrong with that. Being mad is okay. You stay with the emotion and don't make the anger somebody else's fault. If you are mad, that is your feeling. He or she is not creating the anger. It is simply a part of you, who you are at the moment. Allow it to be. See what it feels like. Don't hide away from it; choose it. Play with it. Learn what it means. What does anger really feel like? The same with love; imagine yourself loving. Feel it. Experience it. You own that emotion as well. Nobody creates that within you. It is yours. You can feel it whenever you choose. Do this with all of your emotions. Understand how they work. Learn to read yourself. Instead of self-hatred, you will reach self-acceptance. With self-acceptance there is self-compassion.

We may not like some things about ourselves because they do not fit into somebody else's rule book. Perhaps, according to other people, we are too loud, talk too much or are too argumentative. As we accept who we are, patterns of behaviour, of insecurity and trying to fit in will fall away. As self-acceptance becomes stronger, there will be less judgment of ourselves and others, and there will be more inner peace. We could try for one day just to feel and accept ourselves and our emotions without blaming others or ourselves. It is very difficult because of what we believe or have been taught is the truth. Let's throw away other people's rules of behaviour and discover who we are!

When we feel broken, we judge other people to feel better about ourselves. Yet they are human, too. With all of our foibles and fears, our love, our hate, our prejudices and our kindness, we are human. We reflect life in ourselves and cannot be anything else but human. We are exactly who we are supposed to be.

How then do we discover and communicate with ourselves? How do we get what we want in life? We had already decided what we want by creating and changing time and events into stories based on our values and beliefs. As we understand our beliefs and rules created by our beliefs, our experiences change and life takes a different path.

We live the "story" of our lives as though the story is the real and ideal truth. We believe the stories because our life experiences say they are the truth. The human mind wants and needs to know the truth so we can secure tomorrow and be safe from suffering.

We communicate our stories of what life means to us rather than living our dreams because we feel helpless in the face of life's struggles.

The story would not be very good, though, if there was no excitement, so most of us create a thrill here and there. We take risks in sports, in love and in education but still try to do it in a safe environment. We forget that it is not about control as much as it is about our creations – which are most often exciting, energetic and vibrant.

We say that our wants are "unwanted" because they seem unrealistic according to our beliefs. Yet our wants and dreams are the creative drive of all that is, even nice un-useful things like clothes or learning to skate. There are huge motivating forces that have us testing our wings at creation and there is no sitting back to watch life unfold. There is nobody at the wheel except for us. Where do these drives come from and how do we experience them? Our drives seem to start as a whisper in our minds. As we live our lives, those whispers turn to roars pushing us in the direction of where the drive insists on going.

For instance, I had wanted to write this book for twenty years and ignored doing so because I was busy working and raising a family. I had the manuscript partially written and would look at it occasionally but never felt the push towards completion. One day that all changed. I woke up and my mind was alive with ideas for the book and I felt compelled to sit and write. I felt that this book was important and it had to be done.

I know of people who have a drive to travel. They cannot sit still. They have a knapsack always ready, in case the mood strikes them and away they go! Just like that!

Life is certainly varied with how it pushes us into different directions.

Ironically, at the same time, we like to think of ourselves as unique individuals. We believe that we have free will and that god is part of us rather than the other way around. That idea came from Judaism where they say that since man's soul is part of god, that part is free to choose since all the rest of us has been decided by god. Funnily enough, that is a tautology - god is part of us because of a divine soul and we are part of god because god decides for us about life.

Imagine being divine and accepting our responsibility for what we create and not making it someone else's fault. Imagine that by accepting who we are and understanding our humanity, we can change the world. We no longer need to feel helpless and sit on the sidelines.

Rebecca Schofield[35], a seventeen year old girl who lives in New Brunswick, Canada, is dying of brain cancer. She decided to make her time on earth count. She wrote up her bucket list of the things she wanted to do and included a goal of creating "a mass act of kindness." She went on to say that it could be a big or small as you want. It can be a charity, volunteer or even doing dishes when you don't have to.

She started something that was small and it has grown all over Canada and - who knows? - could be influencing the world. All those small acts of kindness were started by Rebecca.

We are not small as individuals. We are as big as life itself and we have the power to experience it fully.

---

[35] http://www.cbc.ca/news/canada/new-brunswick/beccatoldmeto-becca-schofield-riverview-cancer-1.3906585

LETTING GO AND BEING GOD

In his book, *Wine of the Dreamers*,[36] *John D. MacDonald created a world where people dreamed at night of love, violence and poverty. They subsequently found out that their dreaming was influencing another race on a different planet to act out those dreams.*

Imagine applying people's dreams on a universal scale to our world. In our dream of life, we dream of living, loving, suffering and dying, thus creating our global reality. Each one of us has constant mental and emotional chatter. In fact, it is human and we cannot turn it off unless we choose to do so in a meditative state. That chatter is our creativity, our palette and our video addition to the world.

Every single human being is contributing their stories and beliefs in exactly the same creative dynamic as we are. Imagine as well, what it is that we think about. Sometimes it is fun. When we are hungry, we dream of apple pie. That is a delicious addition to the world! When we are excited about seeing a loved one, ripples of that love are added to all of life. When we sing, we add harmony and music to our universal voice. Every single thought, action and deed that we do is part of god's behaviour in our world. We are completely involved and we are creativity at its finest.

We are more than a set of beliefs running around in a body that came from the earth and will go back to the earth, like a clay doll. We are living on a material world as if the world is the truth and our personas and stories of life are the dreams. We don't understand how much our dreams influence our lives and the world.

We speak of faith and visions, but few of us knowingly utilize these

---

[36] Wikipedia. 2006. Wine Of The Dreamers. Last modified December 27, 2016. https://en.wikipedia.org/wiki/Wine_of_the_Dreamers

human qualities to participate in creation. Imagine being taught our responsibility for all that is on earth in Creation 101 in high school. We would look at war, poverty and disease very differently if we each felt personally responsible for how the world functions.

Individuals can collectively respond to the human condition and we can affect the dreams and the direction mankind chooses. By being responsible for ourselves and fulfilling our strongest dreams, we utilize our potential and change our world. We must learn to accept that we are worth those big dreams by acting on them and sharing them with others instead of accepting the safety of anonymity and deference.

Those big dreams are not necessarily about our careers or our families. Gandhi had a dream of a free India, Mark Zuckerberg was a computer tech who loved to talk on the internet and Facebook was born. Mother Teresa helped the poor in India and the Catholic Church made her a saint. These stories and many more are the dreams that millions of people do quietly every day.

Whether it is to help a neighbour, work at a food bank, do our jobs well, help a friend, get our university degree or do whatever drives us, the creativity of all of us resounds and creates our world. What is our potential? It is only when each of us asks that personal question and acts on the answer that we personally create a world that we can live in.

If we believe that there is an Armageddon reality and we are worthless, then that is where the world will go. This is not about positive thinking. This is about accepting the fact that we create by our very nature. We are god living life and that force demands expression.

When we don't believe in ourselves and don't pursue our dreams, it is like a tree being afraid to grow. We become stunted and afraid. We twist our growth potential into distorted shapes in the same way a constantly buffeted tree is contorted by the weather. Imagine a tree saying that it can't grow because it doesn't believe it can or is afraid to.

It is the same natural growth for us to develop our creativity. The risk of acting on our biggest dreams by believing in our abilities is very frightening and makes us feel vulnerable to both failure and success. To risk everything to fulfill our dreams is so scary that we admire those who can do it. We never think that life is about creatively acting out our dreams and the reason we are here. Instead it is easier to trudge along the same dreary road of safety and security and to allow others to be responsible for our lives.

When we talk about dreams, we are also speaking about the unconscious. We think that the conscious is real and the unconscious only happens in our dreams. What if it is the reverse? What if our conscious minds are our dreams and our unconscious minds are real? When we think about our world, doesn't it seem like a nightmare? When we think about our human creativity and our potential, doesn't that feel like an unattainable dream?

When we understand that god is everything, god stops being the loving, kind and wonderful father of Christianity. God is also not the vengeful, vindictive and jealous god of early Judaism. Our concepts and religious stories about god are a mirror version of ourselves in all of our glory and humanity. Each of us contains all the qualities of life and because we are perception creators and story tellers, we choose the parts we want to play.

We need to know what is going on tomorrow, so we can feel safe today. The problem with feeling safe is that our perceptions of the world are part of our story. When we validate ourselves, we only accept the circumstances that agree with us. If there are any flaws or contradictions to our story, we simply and unconsciously don't see them. In this way, we continue to view our reality from our censored story rather than from our responsibility for creation. Ironically, it doesn't matter. Whether we know it or not, we continue to create the world and ourselves because that is who we are.

We would prefer to control god through religion and our reality through blame so that we can be saved from our personal fear of pain and failure. Nobody knows what will happen next. Even though there are no rules in life to keep us safe or make us feel whole, we try to extend control over life so that we can have freedom from fear and want.

In Buddhism and Hinduism, there is a belief in reincarnation, that we return from previous lives in order to work out the error of our ways or karma. In fact, their religions say that we return as many times as necessary until we reach enlightenment or connection with the absolute mind and clear up the past. As a result, devout followers who desire the Buddha try to build up merits in the present life to balance the karma from past lives so they don't have to return again. They hope that their consciousness will again be fully joined with the Absolute in all of eternity. Their rules of behaviour are not only applied to this life but to their past and future lives as well.

As human beings, we have trouble understanding that we are not broken and that we are simply human! We think our thoughts are puny, yet individually and collectively we participate in creating life on earth and it is up to us, collectively, on whether our lives are heaven or hell.

Imagine replacing that broken-and-trying-to-fix ourselves feeling with living, and being excited about exploring the human potential that we are. We could experience each day to the fullest. Each day could be a risk, but it could also be a commitment to being alive and a challenge of self-discovery.

The hardest thing there is to do is with our lives is to let go of fear and embrace creativity. When we fight life to be safe, we suffer tremendously by not experiencing the joy of challenging ourselves to be all that we are. Since we have the responsibility for our creations on this planet, self-control is not required but self-acceptance is. We could drop all of our facades and armour and face the world with who we are. We do this by allowing our pain, our joy, our hope and our fear to be experienced and not hidden away. This is what it means to be fully in the human experience. This is self-acceptance on a grand scale.

Suffering is one doorway to ourselves. That is not to say that suffering is pleasant. It is not and it hurts, but if the purpose for suffering is to discover a way to understand who we are, then we don't need to be stuck with the fear of suffering and can use it to experience our part in the world.

I can remember a day when I was despondent about my life. I decided that rather than running from the feeling I would explore it.

I poured myself a glass of red wine, sat in my office and said to myself, "Nobody loves me. I am alone." This was how I felt. I immediately thought to myself, "I can call my daughter and she will tell me she loves me." I decided instead to stay with the feeling. I tried to go deeper into the feeling to understand what despondency meant. I wanted to get to the crux of it. Then I thought, "I can call my friend, she will tell me she loves me." Once again I decided to stay with the feeling. Ten minutes later, my mind was bored with the feeling of despondency and switched to another thought and other feelings ensued.

If I had bought into the story of despondency, I could have found a lot of reasons to feel sorry for myself. What creates the feelings though?

That is what is interesting. It is in our self-exploration that we discover the mechanics of our lives.

Happily, we are human and as a species, we are a living gestalt of life. So, when I say that we are the creator, it means that we create our own reality from our conscious and unconscious wants and desires, even if at times, they are no fun. As well, when we act from our self-awareness, we can understand that we are doing our lines from our lives and that all of creation is our stage.

When we believe that we personally control god, we cause trouble because of our religious beliefs, such as the Catholic Inquisition or witch burning. When we accept that we are god, (which ironically is considered the greater egotism), we are filled with god. That's all there is. When we fully accept our godhood and are one with all that is we are whole and complete. That doesn't make us happy all the time or even successful by our cultural standards but since we have this one life to live, why are we doing it in fear?

Experiencing being god is tough to comprehend. We come closest to feeling the divine when we have no sense of self. This is not about running out to lose our self-identities but about attaining a sense of no-self through interacting with life fully. For example, when we look at a beautiful sunset there is a sense of totality, a relaxation within and a trust that all is right in the world. Happily, being a part of the beauty makes us want more of the oneness experience. We long for the feeling of wholeness once again and that drives us towards self-transcendence.

As we let go of trying to repair ourselves, we find serenity. It is a "Catch-22" situation.

In order to discover our humanity, we have to accept our unhappiness when we are sad and feeling broken. As we get used to the idea of being divine, we also have to accept our right to joy, peace and happiness without looking over our shoulders to see what life is going to throw at us next.

We have only one life. When we observe life outside of ourselves, we create a we/they situation. We, of course, all think the same way compared to those others, who don't think correctly at all. All those others such as dust, dirt, worms, rain, bugs and people that are not we, are troublesome and perceptually unacceptable to living a happy and satisfying life. Since *we* are all of this life, there is no other anything to make a *they*. Reality is not about us and them. Everything and everyone exists as part of the *we*.

We believe we are separate and alone trapped in our bodies and subject to old age and disease. However, because we have insight and intuition we can learn to use those skills to have glimpses into the universal.

As we increase our glimpses, we feel more one with god and our sense of loneliness and separation begins to disappear. Whether we live on after death or come back from bad karma becomes irrelevant as our daily life becomes more interesting and full.

We have only one life to live. We are all part of the we.

Creation is vital and alive. Just like people.

HOW TO BE CREATIVE

Creation, by its very definition, is an energetic force that manifests into reality various shapes, forms, ideas, thoughts and actions. Creation is vibrant, alive, and full of promise and vitality, just like people.

By nature, humans create all the time with our thoughts and stories that we repeat endlessly to ourselves. We do this from the time we are born until the time we die. We pile up stories, beliefs and thoughts. Some of these constructs get buried and others become enhanced.

For instance, if I am told that I am smart as a child and then I do well in school, it reinforces my belief in my intelligence and I apply for jobs that require intelligence. I look for people who are equal to me and I have expectations of where my life should go. As life goes on, I discover that there are many people who are smarter than me. This affects my self-confidence and when I don't get the career advancements that I think I should, I feel like a failure. The belief began when I was told I was smart and I didn't have the objectivity to understand that intelligence is relative. I may be smart in some things but sure am dumb in others!

This is just one example of a belief. We have beliefs and stories about everything and we reinforce them constantly. In fact, when we try not to think, it is difficult. To just sit and enjoy a cup of coffee or watch the grass grow without our judgment, memories, beliefs and stories interpreting what is going on, requires practice. We are so used to our minds deciphering the world that we never think our deciphering or mental filter is a form of self-hypnosis.

When we go to sleep at night, we dream about our beliefs with our unconscious minds and we are not aware that our beliefs manifest our perception of reality.

For instance, I want to win a marathon. I practice during the day and at night I have a dream of running and a man hands me a bag of gold along the way. When I wake up, I feel excited and I'm sure that I will win the marathon. I enhance my training and I feel great. I am so sure that I am going to win, my confidence builds and on the day of the race I come in first.

My dreaming about the man with the bag of gold affected my performance.

How do we learn about who we are through our beliefs and stories? How do we learn to use our creativity so that we are not on autopilot governed by fear and uncertainty?

We learn about ourselves through observation, mindfulness, meditation, journaling, painting, socializing and living. Part of our self-observation is learning to accept and work with all our emotional parts of us. A good example of this is the Disney movie called *Inside Out*. It is about an eleven-year-old girl named Riley who lives in Minnesota. The movie personifies five different emotions: Joy, Anger, Fear, Sadness and Disgust. Each of these core emotions have their own personalities which affect Riley.

In the movie, Joy has boundless energy and enthusiasm for life. She loves to solve problems and it is a joy to be around her. She believes sadness is a burden to be pushed out of sight. Joy is unstoppable, amazing and a constant optimist.

Anger feels everything very deeply. He is intense, passionate and proactive. He is bossy and in a hurry to get things done even if they are not done correctly.

Fear is a worrier and a planner. He is the organizer and has planned for all the possible outcomes. He is the key to self-preservation.

Disgust loves her social status. She knows who's who, what to wear at the right time and who to hang out with. She is cool and says the truth as she sees it.

Sadness knows that there is pain in life. She doesn't avoid pain because she knows it could be detrimental to her well-being. Sadness knows life is hard but you can't grow without adversity.

In the end, they all have to learn to work together to help Riley in her move to a new home. It is an interesting movie to watch because it shows dramatically how our emotions and beliefs are developed at a young age and how they affect us.

A good visualization exercise you could use to explore your various emotions is called *The Boardroom*. To do this, visualize a boardroom where all the parts of yourself are present. Take time to actually look at each part. Notice how many board members you have and which board members are male or female. See how each board member is dressed and how they are feeling. If you have something you are trying to resolve or do, ask the board if they agree to what you want. If some dissent, ask why. Learn how to speak with your board. Discuss with your board how you can reconcile problem areas. Get their input and agreement on how you want to function. Just as in the *Inside Out* movie, your board is a compilation of your emotions and beliefs and just as in the movie, you function better when all your parts work together.

Journaling is another good method to understand who you are and what you want in life. It is not a diary but a method of talking to yourself to define and discuss problems, worries, life or relationships. I find that journaling gives me clarity and answers. Neal Donald Walsch wrote a book called *Conversations with God,* which was basically journaling his frustration to god and getting answers back. Try that method. You could get interesting results.

As well, we can explore our unconscious through our dreams, learn what our symbols mean to us and perhaps write our dreams so that we understand the world of our unconscious.

We question every single part of our lives to understand if we are looking at life through personal lenses or a reality we have never seen or explored beyond our constructs of life. Who knows what the world looks like without our beliefs? Imagine what it would be like to understand how each one of us represents the human race.

It would be similar to a body cell. Each cell, for example, a skin cell, represents a system. Although they appear undifferentiated, each cell is extremely important to the integrity of the body. We know this because rogue cells are called cancer.

It is the same with us; when we are in balance and creating things, our societies and the earth are healthy and in harmony. The opposite can also be true. We create no matter what, but if we have no compassion for our lives and we believe our terrible self-stories, we can affect the health and beauty all around us, including our environment, each other and our global population.

When we look at the world, we believe that we need peace and co-operation in order to have a place that is habitable for future generations and ourselves. We imagine that all countries can get along and that all people should have enough to eat. We create global associations like the United Nations so that all nations can be equal and can help countries that are in distress. At the same time, we fear our neighbours, people with different skin colour, losing our jobs, being all alone and dying terrible deaths.

We believe, with all of our hearts, in peace and yet it is difficult to have compassion for ourselves and each other. If we cannot create this peace for ourselves and we represent humanity in the world, then how can this peace be attainable globally?

As a common creation scenario, imagine lacking in something that creates fear, money to pay rent, for instance. If there is no money to pay rent, then we will lose our place, and all our stuff will end up on the street. Somewhere at this point the rest fades into blankness as our minds become so afraid that we stop thinking about our stressors and shift to something more comfortable. At this point, we stuff our fear onto our mental back burner, where it becomes part of the boogieman.

When we don't let the fear stop us, and we continue the story, our minds will *always* end up in the positive as opposed to the fear. So as the story continues, we ask ourselves, "What happens when we are on the street?" Take each fear to the nth degree by asking "What happens next?" "We end up on the street and will have to sleep in the cold, and eat at the food bank."

Perhaps we will be cold and hungry and then someone will give us a blanket. The person becomes our friend and we learn to panhandle together. From panhandling we move to working in a store and perhaps going back to school and from there we have our own corporation and make millions.

Observe where the mind balks at the story and tries to stop or change the subject. Don't give in to fear. Instead, keep asking, "What happens next?" and keep going until the fear story starts to change. Fear stops us from thinking further. We don't want fear and when we stay with our story, our mind shifts. We are so used to believing our fear stories and letting them stop us, we don't know that our fear stories can become success stories.

None of these stories are the truth until we create them by absolutely believing our stories. They are just stories we tell ourselves based on our history and culture until we believe them into our material reality.

Believing our stories is the key to changing what we say to ourselves about reality. We can tell ourselves, till the cows come home, happy stories, but if we don't believe them, how can we change our minds? Since we believe whatever our minds have been trained to tell us, it becomes an exercise in retraining our minds. We have to start small with little things we can believe and once we accept the little things, we can grow those little things into bigger beliefs and eventually we change our minds and are able to go forward with our new beliefs.

How about another for-instance? We lose all our money and can't pay the rent. We are out on the street and cold and hungry. Along comes a very rich person who immediately falls in love with us and we live happily ever after.

Our minds cannot be idle. They are story machines perpetually envisioning reality. They create story after story *and we pick and choose which ones to focus on based on what we believe in.* It is not a matter of positive or negative but the mechanics of how we think.

Ironically, we believe our fear stories faster than we believe our hope and happiness stories. If we get stung by a bee, the phobia is instantaneous. If we win the lottery, we want more and are afraid of the loss of the money.

Fear is a powerful emotion. The opposite of fear is something called loving-kindness.

The term loving-kindness is our human-to-human expression of love. It has been called many names in various philosophies and religions, including Judaism, Buddhism, Christianity, Hinduism and Jainism. This is a form of love exhibited by acts of kindness. In Judaism it is characterized by the core commandment as "Love thy neighbour as thyself."[37]

In Buddhism loving-kindness is called Mettā. It is practiced as a meditation to cultivate good will towards self and others.

We can live with and overcome fear by practicing loving-kindness. We can create our own loving-kindness meditation to believe in ourselves and to find meaning in our lives. As we practice loving-kindness for ourselves, we are able to extend it to other people.[38]

This practice was originally taught by the Buddha to his some of his monks who became frightened while meditating in the forest. They heard strange noises while in the woods and asked the Buddha for help

---

[37] Holy Bible. 1959. Leviticus 19:18.

[38] Wikipedia, 2016. "Mettā." Last modified May 5, 2017. https://en.wikipedia.org/wiki/Mett%C4%81

with their fear of the noises. Buddha taught them the loving-kindness meditation and told them to go back into the woods and practice this with the spirits who were creating the noise. The story goes on to say that the monks did return to the forest, made friends with the spirits through the loving-kindness meditation and stayed a long time in the woods.

Here are some phrases to choose from to create your own loving-kindness meditation. This list is not exhaustive and can be added to with whatever you need to help balance your fear with love. Choose which ones you like. You can use other phrases if they sound better to you. Try using three or four together as a chant or mnemonic phrase for when you are suffering or afraid:

May I be free from fear. May I be happy. May I be full of hope. May I be free to love. May I be full of compassion. May I forgive myself. May I love my body. May I have compassion for myself. May I be free. May I be free of suffering. May I be one with god. May I experience all that is.

As part of the Buddhist meditation, which includes others:

May you be happy and fulfilled. May you be free from fear. May you be one with god. May you be free from suffering.

Lastly, as part of the complete meditation, which includes everybody:

May all beings be free from suffering. May all beings be happy and fulfilled. May all beings have compassion for themselves. May all beings forgive themselves.

This loving-kindness meditation can be used anywhere at any time whenever we need help, calmness, compassion towards ourselves or others, or simply when feeling down or unhappy. This can also be turned into a meditation ritual at home, at work or in a group.

So a completed meditation could look like this:

May I be free from suffering. May I be free from fear. May I be happy and compassionate to myself and others.

May you be free from suffering. May you be free from fear. May you be happy and compassionate to yourself and others.

May all beings be free from suffering. May all beings be free from fear. May all beings be happy and compassionate to themselves and others.

It is suggested that we use the meditation for ourselves until we feel comfortable enough to care for others.

There is no positive or negative story. What we believe in and focus on is how we perceive our reality. Remember the story of the lollipops in a candy store? If all we believe in are lollipops, that is all that we will see.

The purpose of thinking and storytelling is to keep us safe from the fear about the unknown tomorrow. As a habit of thought, we believe that tomorrow is not an uncontrollable reality if we can visualize, feel, touch, hear and imagine it. We believe that if we don't worry about tomorrow, it may not exist.

It is the same conundrum of one hand clapping and whether or not we hear it; or the riddle of the tree falling in the forest. Does it make a noise if we are not present? If we don't mentally create a tomorrow, will there be one?

The outside world can harm or devastate us in ways that we worry about, but we believe if we counter the worry with logic and planning, we will be safe. If that were true, there would never be any car accidents, unemployment, theft or other disasters. It would be easier for us to understand how to flow with life rather than worrying about what will happen next.

Try this exercise for one week: don't think about tomorrow. Obviously, if your child is needed at a sports activity, that has to be planned but for yourself, don't plan. Be involved in everything as it happens. Watch what your mind does, how it works at telling you a story of what is going to happen if you do this or that. Maybe if you don't worry the sky will fall in, maybe it won't. It's a tough choice about whether to worry or not.

To let go of fearing tomorrow and to trust your right to be here requires great courage.

Our fear of tomorrow is based on our mind's perception that we will not exist unless we think into the future. In order to let go of fearing tomorrow, we have to be able to accept our own death. To accept our own death, we need to feel that we are completely part of life. It is the conundrum of living. In order to be at peace, we have to be fully alive and in tune with everything around us. Our creative ability is our gift to experience life. We use the stuff of life - energy in order to create. As we use our creator skills such as visualizing, storytelling and dreaming to appreciate our lives, we can live moment to moment without fear of ending.

We paint ourselves a future and then we react to that future as though it were the truth. If I believe that I will win the lottery and it doesn't occur anytime, I feel like a failure. Perhaps a simpler way would be to let life unfold.

Another alternative to our worry and fear stories is to catch ourselves in the worry and understand that our stories are talking about lack and danger. Since we know that we can shift our story any way we want to, we can try shifting it to abundance and freedom. This is simply doing mental reframing and as we become more practiced and the habit of thinking about abundance becomes easier, we may notice that we worry less and life starts changing. We become more aware of all of life's experiences instead of just lack or danger.

Michael Talbot wrote a book called *The Holographic Universe* where he suggests that the world is really a hologram[39], just like the holographic deck on the *Starship, Enterprise.* On the starship's holodeck, the crew could live out a completely different experience than their daily life on board the ship.

In our holographic world, reality is more fluid and interwoven than we believe.

For instance, I have a friend who had trouble making a decision about her life so she looked around her and observed an eagle flying overhead. She imagined that she was dreaming and asked herself what the dream meant. To her, the eagle symbolized freedom and happiness and she chose the path in life that meant freedom to her.

A symbol is a metaphor that stands for something else, something real. When we dream of a rock, we don't say, "This is a rock in our dream." We say, "What does that rock mean?" How do we define rock? What do we feel about rock? Is rock permanent or will it explode? In other words, we ask ourselves questions about the rock in an enquiring fashion. We don't say "bad rock." We question what the rock represents.

The same is true even with nightmares. We don't ask ourselves literally why the boogieman in our dreams scares us; it is more that we want to know what fear the dream symbolizes. Even a bleed-through or daydream where there is an "Ah hah!" moment is symbolic of greater meaning.

Everyday life can be examined in the same way as a dream for its metaphors. We are dreaming about life on autopilot rather than consciously participating in life's creation.

[39] Talbot, M. The Holographic Universe. 1991. HarperCollins Publishers. New York. NY: USA

Think about some of the metaphors we use on a daily basis. Here are a few: Life is just a bowl of cherries. Is that a chicken or egg argument? You just let the cat out of the bag. You look three sheets to the wind. That is the snowball effect. We are at the point of no return.

We understand all the meanings of the metaphors and don't take them literally. If we were dreaming about snowballs, we could understand that we should look for a cascading event. When we are awake, the metaphors still exist. We are simply not used to deciphering them when we are awake. The more we practice interpreting life as a dream, the more we feel like we belong because of our interacting with life's events.

As human beings, we create our lives every second of the day. We do it naturally and without effort. We wake up in the morning and the day simply begins! Our minds kick in, telling us who we are, what the day will bring us, what to be afraid of and what our dreams for the future are. We create with a different part of ourselves at night and we say our night dreams aren't real even though we can be affected by them. We create stories of oceans and we make friends with the fish. The next year we create different stories and we eat those same fish.

We create unconsciously and consciously, continuously and fruitfully in every part of our lives with our beliefs and our stories. We never ask ourselves how we actually make our creations. *In fact, we are not even aware that we are daily, minute by minute, living inside our creations as though they were the truth.* All of this is done in the name of purposeful living!

Telling stories about our lives is part of our creativity. That is the joy of our myths, fairy tales and movies. It is not a fault to be gotten rid of. Our stories, both when we are awake and when we are dreaming, let us experience living. When we dream, we accept the story as symbolic of life. Life is symbolic of our god experience.

When people dream, they believe there is a separation between their dreaming and the reality of the present world. There is no difference. Dreaming is about all of our parts coming together to joyfully play at creation. This is the ground of all new ideas and creations in the world. When we interpret our dreams, we read how the world is going. In our dreams, we are given all the information about us and our world. We also receive this information through hunches and intuition but the trick is to expand our ability to be consciously aware of what we are creating globally.

When we are dreaming, our beliefs through our collective unconsciousness are part of the creativity of our world.

Listen to your intuition. Listen to the metaphors you use regularly and you will learn to interpret the world as though you are dreaming it. From there you can understand your creativity and be active rather than reactive.

For example, one day I was walking down a street to my home. A truck drove by with some baby stuff in it and I thought to myself, "Okay, that is my childhood passing me by." As I continued down the road some teenagers passed me, giggling and laughing as teenagers are wont to do and I said to myself, "So these are my teen years that are passing me." As I continued walking down the road, I came to a bushy corner, which I usually turned at. Suddenly, I began to worry about muggers. I got so scared I began to tell myself to wake up. Here I was, 10:30 in the morning, out walking down a street and I was telling myself to wake up!

I told myself I was foolish - to turn the corner and I would see that nobody was there. Well! When I turned the corner about one hundred yards down the road, standing right in the middle of the road, was a man who looked exactly like what I believed a mugger would look like.

It scared me so much I went and hid behind a tree. Again, I told myself to wake up and not be foolish.

I told myself that when I went back to the street, the man would be a long way down and walking away from me. I tentatively went back to the street and the man was nowhere to be found! He was gone!

It was an interesting experience. Not only had I been uncertain if I was dreaming or awake, but the metaphors popped themselves into my perceptual reality!

The divide between being awake and dreaming while we are sleeping is a subtle interface between our conscious-belief daytime awareness and our metaphor-creating, reality-developing unconscious sleep awareness.

Another great exercise to try when we are awake, is to tell ourselves that we are asleep and dreaming and when we go to bed at night, suggest to ourselves that we are waking up.

As we develop this, the divide between the conscious and unconscious mind becomes less and the world becomes a different place. Perhaps this is where Harry Potter and super-heroes fit in.

We can interpret our everyday lives as though they are a dream. Perhaps we could even become so skilled with it, creation becomes obvious. There is no divide between what we believe and what we perceive. It is in our conscious awareness of being alive that we can play at living our dreams.

In the world, life is perfect when we take away our judgment about life, even as we work at accepting ourselves for who we are. We understand the philosophy yet in our minds we want to control what we don't like. Perhaps this is an inkling of our being god. Then we forget that inkling and try to hedge our bets by negotiating with god, the universe, or whatever we believe is our higher power.

We are not certain that we are included as part of life and so to stave off that uncertainty, we search for and try to create certainty in our lives. This gives us a thin veneer of stability over an apparently unstable reality. After all, we really don't know what is going to happen tomorrow.

It's hard to imagine giving up control and *trusting in ourselves* that we belong here and being at peace with whatever happens. That is ultimate peace. There is no how-to-do this, as the how is invested in maintaining the fiction that there is something to control. So it is more *how-not*-to-do this.

We could stop trying to be more of anything and discover who we are right now. We have the power to utilize all of creation in our dreams, stories and beliefs. For instance, if we choose to live our lives by being a plumber, then nothing on this planet will get in the way of that.

On the other hand, since we are experiencing life, things can change. Nothing remains the same forever. Otherwise, it becomes boring. For instance, try hanging on to an emotion for longer than five or ten minutes. It is impossible. Our emotions shift and move.

While we are awake, we believe fervently that this material world is the only truth. Our world actually is a large gestalt of energy, turning human dreams into perceptual reality. Humanity dreams of hope, despair, wants and needs because we are the creators and not the recipients of divine grace.

When we bump a table, it hurts; when we stay too long in the sun, we burn. Our senses relay stimulation from our physical environment telling us how our world looks, feels and sounds. Or does it? First of all, stimulation enters our senses and gets interpreted by our brain. The brain uses our beliefs and life experiences to define what our senses tell us. So, for example, if we don't believe in the colour green, we simply won't see it. Also, if our brain is damaged in various parts, it would change our experience of the world. Sights, smells, behaviour and emotions are all affected.

In other words, there is no objective physical world out there that we interact with. Rather, the world as we understand it is deeply personal.

Remember the story of the three blind men and an elephant? One blind man felt the tail and said that the elephant is long and thin. The second blind man disagreed and said the elephant was large and like the side of a building. The third blind man said no, the elephant is like a long, thick, rubbery snake. All three blind men had a view of the elephant from their own perception!

Did you ever play that falling back game of trusting that there was someone there to catch you when you were falling? The truth is sometimes there is and sometimes there is not. It is by trusting in that ambiguity that there is a sense of wholeness. There is a confidence inside of you that no matter what, you will be all right.

It is by letting go of security and the need for reassurance that relaxes us and allows us to let go of the known boundaries of self. This is called faith in who we are. It is a huge risk to give up our beliefs about our personal selves and it is enough to send most people back to the crowd with a sigh of relief - into the known reality of everyday life.

We cannot understand tomorrow with our minds. That is not the part of us that is creating. Instead, we can use our minds to appreciate what our creative self does. We explore ourselves by creating self-images to discover what happens next. We create stories about who we are and we add to the consciousness of the world through our individual experiences. For each human being, there is a different reality and thus together we create a diverse and complex view of life functioning, just like an orchestra.

To understand how we create our lives we listen to the space between words and feel the meaning behind the symbols of our consciousness. We listen to the voice behind the voices that tell us who we are. We discover who we are as a life experience and make it a daily practice.

We need to direct all of our will and energy to get through the static of mental activity and be obsessive with the desire to know ourselves. If there are any doubts, the personal stories that we create will continue to be our truth.

Our experiences create possibilities for tomorrow
and for acceptance of life and death.

THE GROUND OF ALL EXISTENCE

The question of how an outside god participates in the world has been a dialogue since man first had to deal with questions of the hereafter. The god who sits in heaven does not fit into our world view today, because an outside god makes no objective sense in our Age of Reason. With our knowledge of astronomy and physics, it is pretty clear there is no such physical area as heaven or hell out there somewhere.

Karen Armstrong wrote in her book, *The History of God*, that when she began her research of religion she expected god to be a projection of human needs and desires. She discovered that, while there was some truth to that, it was not completely true. She said that when she consulted with respected spokespeople from all three monotheistic religions, they told her that instead of waiting for god to come down from on high, it was better to create a sense of god for herself. She went on to say that while god did not exist out there, "He" was the most important reality in the world.[40] Armstrong suggested that Homo Sapiens should change their species name to Homo Religiosus because we feel the need for god.

Paul Tillich was a theologian from the 1950's who was critical of the view that god was a supreme-being or presence. He felt that if god were a being, god could not be called the source of all-being, since who would have created god? Instead, he suggested that god should be understood as the "ground of being-itself."

Tillich said that since there is only being alive (where we and our world exist - as opposed to non-being), there is a power of being. He saw god as the ground upon which all beings exist. God is everything. This includes

---

[40] Armstrong, Karen. A History Of God. http://www.metaphysicspirit.com/books/A%20History%20of%20God.pdf

this world and the cosmos, both macroscopically and microscopically. As such, god is life itself.

When Tillich talked about the ground of being, he didn't know about quantum field theory.

In chapter two, I described how an atom was made of electrons orbiting a nucleus, (which was made up of smaller particles called quarks). Atoms make up base chemicals, which then form molecules and then eventually form all of life, including us. Photons (light particles) are the energy source that changes the movement of electrons into various molecules. Photons are waves (just like light rippling in water) until they bump into electrons where they turn into particles to move the electrons.

Everything in the universe is made up of vibrating quantum and electron fields. These vibrations create harmonic resonances, just like a flute, for instance. As you blow the flute it changes tones based on air pressure pushed through the flute's holes. Harmonic resonance is measured in hertz or repeating wavelengths of frequencies created by the vibrations.

Our brains are run by various groupings of nerve cells, all interacting with each other and generating an overall electrical field. In fact, our entire bodies have an electric field. Anywhere there's a nerve cell, there's electricity. The electric wave patterns that make up our brain waves are the same equations governing the electromagnetic spectrum, light, particles and everything else in the universe. The light seen coming from a star and the energy of our minds are one and the same type.

The electrical patterns in our brains are called brain waves. They are divided into infra-low frequency waves at .5 hertz, delta frequency waves from .5 to 3 hertz, theta frequency waves from 3 to 8 hertz, alpha frequency waves from 8 to 12 hertz, and beta frequency waves from 12 to 38 hertz.

Our thoughts and dreams are created in this electrical/brain wave field. The thoughts we think, the words we say to ourselves and the dreams we experience are electrical impulses that can be measured by an electroencephalograph machine. Everything about quantum mechanics that describes how electrons and photons behave, applies to our thoughts. This includes the particle-wave duality, superposition (Schrodinger's cat can be dead or alive at the same time depending on the impersonal observer) and entanglement.

Our bodies are like every other groups of particles and photonic energy. Therefore, we are entangled with everything we've ever encountered or will encounter: the environment around us and the rest of the universe.

Entanglement is like ripples in the ocean or what can be imagined as a sea of energy. When we have thoughts or dreams, our electrical impulses create ripples in the sea that come in contact with other people's ripples and other quantum ripple events in life, such as winning the lottery, having a baby, swimming a river, climbing a mountain, feeding chickens and all other life events. Since we are entangled with our environment, we can affect events as well be influenced by the randomness of life with the intersection of ripples, just like in the ocean.

Before we can transition into sleep at night, we need to feel calm, whole and together. In order to do this, our brains shift from fully-awake beta brainwaves to slowing-down alpha brainwaves, then slower to calm-and-at-peace theta brainwaves. Then we fall asleep and shift to delta waves or deep-sleep and dreaming. Our brains transition into wakefulness by reversing our brain waves.

In 1952 a physicist named Winfried Otto Schumann predicted mathematically that the space between the earth and the top of our ionosphere has a harmonic resonance that vibrates at around 7.83 hertz.

The vibrations between our alpha and theta waves (the transition between waking and sleeping) are between 7 and 8 hertz, similar to our planet's harmonic frequency. *We have the same vibrations as the planet earth when we are transitioning between waking and sleeping. How is that for a coincidence?*

This happens naturally before we fall asleep at night and when we first wake up in the morning. In fact, we cannot fall asleep until we get that sense of calmness, as though we have to plug into our energy source before we can re-generate, exactly like the Seven of Nine personality in the show *Star Trek, Voyager.*

Theta brain waves create a state of very deep relaxation and occur during meditation as well. The theta state is also called our subconscious, which mediates between our conscious and unconscious mind. When we feel mystical or spiritual, in touch with god and one with everything, it is during our theta brain wave activity. Every night and every morning we naturally transition through our theta experience going from our delta brainwave deep-sleep state back up to our wide-awake, going-for-it beta brainwaves. No wonder we pray at night before we sleep. We pass god on the way to sleep. In the morning, when we wake up feeling relaxed, we have to say hi to god on the way back to our physical world.

What is real, our dreaming state or being awake? When we go to sleep do we wake up to our creative potential? If we combine our waking and sleeping states do we understand infinity? If life is not symbolic of anything whether we are asleep or awake, then what is life? What if our conception of a higher self is the combination of our theta-delta dream states and our alpha-beta waking states?

Trying to describe or define this combined state of awareness is an individual experience of infinity. Everybody would experience the ground of being differently, in the same way we have individual fingerprints. There is not one size that fits all.

If we searched ourselves to locate where the god part is in our bodies, there would be no such thing. It is throughout our whole being. In fact, the more we search for the god feeling within us, the more we realize that it is the reverse. When we experience the feeling of serenity and oneness, our beliefs, truths, perceptions and fears of life disappear and we discover that there really is no sense of self as our base.

We make every effort to be part of our materialistic world but inevitably we come back to some sort of prayer in our darkest hour or moment of greatest joy. It is while praying, meditating or daydreaming, that our brains utilize our theta brainwaves to help us in our despair, enhance our joy or feel spiritually connected to god.

It turns out that the reality of our subatomic universe really is the ground of being-itself.

All of life is a moving, creative sea of energy manifesting physical stuff into our classical mechanical reality. We are so used to thinking that we are physical beings, it is difficult to imagine those energy forces being us as well as everything else.

Since we are part of the ground of existence, not only are we the creators of our lives through thinking and actions but we are also the experiencers because we are part of life. We tend to think that we are separate entities from the ground of being, and differentiated from all the rest of the planet's species. Yet, at the subatomic level of particles and waves, we are one and the same.

Chaos Theory, also known as the butterfly effect, is one of those anomalous realities that belie reason and objectivity. The phrase was coined by Edward Lorenz in 1972 when he asked "Does the flap of a butterfly's wings in Brazil set off a tornado in Texas?" The answer mathematically was yes. Lorenz was a meteorologist who studied weather patterns. He set up data on his computer and to his surprise, patterns emerged as a constant.

Chaos theory is the mathematical study of apparently random events such as weather and climate. As well, it shows up in traffic patterns, coastline topography, meteorology, economic conditions, sociology and physics. What the theory really means is that events, or places such as coastlines are actually patterns. We have trouble seeing them objectively due to the length of time involved or the size of the pattern.

The patterns of what would normally be called chaos show that even though events and things appear to be random, they are not.

When we experience chaos in our lives, we don't understand which patterns are developing based on time. Our experience of time is faster than the developing patterns moving from chaos to completion. Imagine, during our chaotic times, that each decision that we are making is like a small whirlpool of energy. Each decision is like a weather event. It could occur or not. We don't know. In time, one little chaotic whirlpool decision coalesces into another chaotic whirlpool decision until finally there is only one decision. This is similar to the way that hurricanes and tornadoes are created.

We believe that when we are experiencing chaos that we have to decide what to do. We worry and struggle with the right decision, but when we are in chaos, that is what it is. Chaos is like a pregnant pause, sorting a part of our life into our next pattern. How can we understand what is going on while we are in chaos? It takes time and perspective in order to see the whole picture.

Chaos and the resulting decision are part of the ground of being. Everything is vibrating in harmony within the infinite ground of being.

Chinese medicine uses energy meridians for healing and Ayurveda medicine from India believes in the delicate balance of mind, body and spirit. These functional healing models have been around for thousands of years. The ancient healing modalities utilize our fundamental being (energy) as opposed to Western medicine and the use of pharmaceuticals which bases treatments on the theory that the human body is a machine. Through research of the placebo effect and psychoneuroimmunology, we are discovering that the ancient healing models are better equipped to work with our human psyche. Every day our psychology is translated into our biology.

In the materialist world that we know of today, science has started talking about multiverses rather than just a single one. We go further and further into the universe and cannot see the end. We have no idea if there is an end to the big bang expanding, because while we can see the almost to the beginning of the bang, we don't know what is outside of it. This is infinity. We can only imagine infinity as something large without edges that holds everything in it.

If we consider that we exist within infinity, can we reach into the infinite for creative expression? Elon Musk, Bill Gates and Mark Zuckerberg would probably say so. When we put boundaries on our possibilities and dreams, we block our potential due to our beliefs and fears. We limit our ability to experience our combined waking and dreaming states within the field of being. If we could drop our boundaries and change our beliefs, we would experience creation in all of its glory.

We put walls of doubts around us, denying the infinite possibilities of life experience we could have. That is how we feel alone: with blocks and walls. What does it feel like to have no blocks or walls? Imagine feeling like there is no separation from us with the air, the trees, the bears, the bees, the dirt, the sky and everything else that exists on our world.

We use our beliefs, customs, culture, fears, dreams and hopes to perceive a life for ourselves. We don't imagine that our world view itself could be an illusion. Do we look at our lives and say, "Wow, I created that!" No, we don't. We immediately feel that we are out of control when we examine our lives and hope that someone else with greater authority can fix our lives for us.

In Viktor Frankl's book, *Man's Search for Meaning*, he describes how even in the depths of a concentration camp, people craved living. To survive, though, they had to change their perception of life. Instead of asking why life was so cruel to them, they asked what life wanted from them. It changed their focus so that they could live through their terrible experiences. They felt they owed something to life in order to follow their dreams.

One man believed that there was a girl waiting in another country for him and that he had to have courage to live for her. Another man said that he still had books on science to write and he needed the faith and dedication to live so he could finish his books.

We look at life through the eyes of our beliefs and stories. Since we have the ground of all existence to play in, why choose to think small? We could be our biggest dreams on a global level, and when we believe in ourselves, we could change our perception of who we are and the sky is the limit! Sometimes life is simply about believing in ourselves. Imagine if each one of us asked what life wanted from us!

I once knew a man who, as a teen, was charged with juvenile rape. Tom was innocent but went to jail anyway. When he got out, he was no longer afraid of society because he saw that society's rules were faulty. He decided to challenge fate and create his own rules about life. Tom eventually owned his own logging company, had a beautiful wife and was at peace with his own creations.

We don't need to go to jail for self-discovery because our perceptions and beliefs are already our own prison. Imagine what it would be like to be free.

The only jail bars are in our minds.

Without our truths, our lives would not be the same. Imagine having amnesia. How would we know who we are? We would have no personal opinions or history and we would behave differently.

In the 2012 movie, *The Vow*, Paige (Rachel McAdams) and Leo (Channing Tatum) were in a horrific car accident. Paige woke up with amnesia and didn't remember her husband, Leo. Paige and Leo were happy and in love but after her accident she thought her husband was her doctor. She had no memory of him and didn't believe him when he told her they are married. Her last memories were of being in law school, dating a man named Jeremy and living at home with her parents.

As she tried to live in the present and Leo worked at showing her his love for her, her life puzzled her. She didn't know why she left Jeremy, quit law school and never told Leo about her parents.

The movie showed how she returned to her known past. She found out her father had an affair, which was why she never told her husband about her parents. She went back to law school but discovered herself drawing while in classes and learned why she quit school and became an artist. With Jeremy, she learned he had another girl friend that he was ready to give up for her and she realized why she had left him. The end of the movie had her returning to Leo at their old coffee hangout, and they both made a decision to find a new restaurant to be their new place. They started a new life for themselves because without her memories, she had a different view of life.

We don't realize how much our memories and experiences create who we are. Who would we be if we didn't remember our memories and experiences? It is interesting to think how different we would be.

There was a time when people thought the world was flat. There was a time when people believed that the sky above was a dome with heaven on top of it. There was a time when we believed the colour of our skin created human differences. Now we have different beliefs based on our lives and our histories. Imagine living without those beliefs and stories. We could then see our illusions about life and be present in our creation of a new life.

If I was abused, ignored or beaten as a child, I would have a different view of reality than someone who had been treated with respect, love and care. Does that make us any lesser or different as a human being? No!

We are human and we have the inbuilt power of creativity. What our experiences create is a personal point of view about the world and ourselves. How do we challenge it? It is hard to give up our past experiences. We believe our history is who we are, instead of our experiences of life. After all, we have survived our pasts and are able to fit into our everyday lives. Isn't that enough?

The alternative to being enthralled by our beliefs and our past is called freedom. It is the freedom to create our own lives and participate in global consciousness. There is nobody else calling the shots or creating our destinies while we are living our lives. Each and every one of us matter.

What can our experiencing the ground of all existence do for us? Our experiences create possibilities for tomorrow and an acceptance of life and death. If we can have faith in being human, life is neither meaningless nor directionless.

The blocks within our reality are created by us. The removal of our blocks changes our focus to a different reality. It is like choosing to travel to a destination. Very rarely do we just get on the train. Instead we do research. We look at maps, dates, times, prices and destinations that are our most desirable. Then we save money, book tickets, and dream of the destination. When we finally do our journey, we judge whether or not it was worth it.

When we decide to change our outlook, it requires time for the change to come into effect. The required time depends on our strongly-held beliefs of whether or not the destination is worth the risk. Faith in ourselves helps us risk changing without knowing if we will be successful.

Back to the fellow who was charged with rape: he knew beyond a shadow of a doubt that what was in his past was unwanted and he didn't want that past anymore. He reached into the field of existence and not only defined new parameters but he opened up new territories in his experience of his life.

The universal needs and drives we feel are not of the ego but of our natural creativeness. Imagine listening to those drives. What are they saying? Notice how they push to be manifested and how we all have different drives. Where do those drives come from, if not from the ground of being? Try and ignore our drives and feel what happens. Our ignored drives can "drive" us nuts!

We are not separate from each other. We are part of a vast ocean of energy where the multiple little, beautiful, chaotic whirlpools of life are us. We believe we are separate but we are in the ocean of life.

One of the definitions of perfect is that which is complete and contains all the requisite parts. That sums up all-that-is or the ground of being itself. All of the requisite parts are present, including us. When we accept the premise that we are a creative life force, it can be life-altering and change our ideas from being broken to being perfectly human.

Our dreams at night speak to us in symbols.

Absolute Faith

Our dreams at night speak to us in symbols that we try to interpret when we are awake. In fact, dreams are so important that if we are stopped from dreaming over a period of time, we get sick and have severe anxiety. Not only do we dream at night, we daydream, we meditate, we do self-hypnosis and we use inspiration. Over the years, as our culture and world have become more rational and materialistic, we have paid less attention to what goes on in the our unconscious awareness.

Today we watch movies on magic. Harry Potter is a well-known magical character. Many stories and movies are now written about mythological creatures such as vampires, werewolves and mummies. No matter how hard we try, we live in a world that on the surface is scientific but we are at home in the symbolic world of myths and dreams.

We believe more in the "real" world than in our dreams even though it has been shown countless times that our symbols and myths are a great part of our creativity. It has also been shown that our thoughts can create our physiological reality. For instance, self-hatred can lead to illness and death, while miracles have occurred when people were supposed to die and lived instead.

I knew two men, Mike and Stephen, who were both diagnosed with liver cancer at the same time. They were each given three months to live. One died right on time and the other man died three years later. The only difference appeared to be their state of mind. Mike was prepared to die. He felt he had lived a full life. Stephen's family was very important to him and he wanted to live longer because of his love for them.

I also worked with a woman who had a cancerous tumor wrapped around the aorta of her heart. Her doctor gave her three months to live. When I asked Alison what she saw when she closed her eyes and looked at the tumour, she said she saw a spear right through her heart. She believed the spear was put there by her mother and she felt that she had that spear through her heart for years. She managed, in her mind's eye, to pull out the spear and put a golden bandage through her heart. She lived for three more years.

According to the world of science, people die on time, psychosomatic diseases don't exist and placebos aren't real. In actual fact, there is more to us than just the physical or mental modalities. We are a complex mix of our conscious minds, sensory inputs and beliefs combined with our unconscious minds, symbolic inputs and dreams. We simply aren't aware of our complexity and run on autopilot instead of manual control. We do stuff in life and we don't know why or how.

In 1960, there was a research program done on dream deprivation. The dream researchers had eight young men as subjects. By attaching electrodes to their eyelids, the researchers could see when the dreaming REM or rapid eye movement cycle began. These test subjects were awoken fully each time they began to dream to see what effect it would have. After three days of not dreaming, one subject completely quit the program and the rest needed nights of sleep in order to recover from not dreaming. It was discovered that the longer there was dream deprivation, the longer the subjects needed to dream[41] in order to feel calm and normal.

Our unconscious is part of our creative communication with life. We rarely pay attention to that part of us because we live most of our lives with the understanding that the unconscious is basically no more real than our dreams, hunches, intuition, visions and déjà vu experiences.

When Freud first began doing psychological analysis with people, he discovered that all of their neuroses could be described in symbolic language based on their dreams. He described all of the symbols sexually because of the restrained culture he lived in. Carl Jung disagreed with Freud's descriptions of dream symbols and used man's mythic symbols and common heritage beliefs to decipher his clients' problems.

Carl Jung said in his book, *Man and His Symbols*, that life is a battleground and exists with inexorable opposites - day and night, life and death, happiness and misery, good and evil. He said that these opposites are what create religion and the pain of living.

---

[41] http://citeseerx.ist.pasu.edu/viewdoc/download?doi=10.1.1.409.652&rep=rep1&type=pdf

He also stated that when there is suffering, people begin to seek a way to understand the meaning of life and its bewildering experiences. In his work, he found that people felt that it would make a great difference in their lives if they had a positive belief in a meaningful purpose or in god and immortality[42].

Not much has changed in our world since the time of Carl Jung. The complexities of life continue and we still yearn for wholeness. The conversation about god is still unprovable by scientific standards. Yet, we are more than physical objects whose sole duties in life are to spend money by being good consumers and work hard at unfulfilling jobs.

In our awake, mundane world, we believe in our three- dimensional reality and can see the effects of gravity, climate, disease and community. We work at jobs eight or more hours a day, get hungry and eat when we need to and then go home and watch television or read until we go to bed, just to do it all over again the next day.

We never question whether or not this life is a delusion and, if so, what is real. We dream of a better life for ourselves but cannot find the time to break out of the humdrum. Our lives feel so safe and normal, even when we feel unfulfilled or alone.

We never think our dreams, both in the daytime and while sleeping, are our interface with god. Carl Jung called that interface the collective unconscious and said that it is an age-old belief that god speaks to us chiefly through dreams and visions.[43] We have the ability to dream about what we are capable of doing, who we can be, and how we can live fully.

What if it is just that simple? What if it is true that no matter what we call that dreaming force, we are part of it, utilize it and live life unconsciously as much if not more than we know? What if we learned to understand our symbolic language, our dreams and our symbols in life? What if we learned to participate consciously with our unconscious? Why not, for simplicity's sake, exactly as Carl Jung suggested, call the whole thing, god?

Imagine our unconscious as a vast territory that needs exploring. It is large and beautiful yet mysterious. We don't go striding into the trees and

---

[42] Jung, Carl J. 1964. "*Man And His Symbols*". Bantam Doubleday Dell Publishing Group, New York, NY:USA

[43] Jung, Carl. 1964. "*Man and His Symbols*". Bantam Doubleday Dell Publishing Group, New York, NY:USA

know what we are going to find. Rather we scout the territory, find guides and ask questions about the unknown area so that it is less intimidating.

When we become familiar with the territory, the unknown becomes friendly and safe. How do we know the unknowable? We believe that we can. We fake it until we make it. We practice absolute faith in ourselves and if we act in accordance with that faith, slowly the delusion that we are separate and alone will disappear. It is that simple. We say, "I can know myself." When we say this, it sets up the opportunity for asking, "How do I do this?"

Feel it. Try it. "How do I know myself?" Sit for a minute and think about it. Don't rush on reading. There will be some practical answers. There are many books on dream interpretation, metaphors and symbols. This will give some of the language. Yet it will also be our self-knowledge and self-discovery that will give us the insight of how we, as human beings, function. Simply saying "I am" to all our questions about ourselves, as Nisagaddarta Maharaj suggested, might help with our insight.

There will also be an answer if we listen in silence with our hearts as opposed to our heads. The mind is like a race horse: perfect for its task but limited in what it can do. In order to know ourselves, we need to let go of all preconceived notions of who or what god is. What a shock and surprise it is to discover that there is no god outside of ourselves: nobody to worship, nobody to propitiate, and nobody to absolve us of sins. Instead, as we understand our lives, we can discover what life wants from us.

Have fun, dive in. A really great mental exercise for the experience is, wherever we are, to look around and say, "All of this is god." If we are inside, we could say, "The walls are god. The floor is god. The chair I sit on is god. All of this is god. There is no separation between god and me." If we practice this often, we could get through the noise of our disbelief and live our lives with a different awareness.

The separation from other people that we feel drives us to act like we are something less than who we are. We have an urge away from loneliness into togetherness. So we put on our best party face and go out into the crowd looking for love. First we try and please our parents, then our friends and our bosses and all the time this little voice inside of us says, "I don't want to be alone. Please, I don't want to be alone." Then we pray to god and ask for help. We don't know that the chasm we are trying to cross is in our minds and that there is no aloneness or separation. As we grow in self-awareness and develop faith in ourselves, there will be calmness and peace.

Last week, I went to a high school graduation where a young man named Kevin described how he became so well-liked and popular that he was chosen to be class valedictorian. He described his early years when his parents divorced and how he felt lonely and displaced. He became a loner and angry and thus even more isolated from his peers. He tried to fit in, tried to make friends but his lack of self-confidence got in the way. One day, in desperation he asked his mother what he could do to become popular. She said to him, "Fake it until you make it."

Kevin said that advice changed his life. He said that when he entered any classroom, he went in with a smile. He helped anyone who needed it. He was always cheerful and friendly with everyone. In time, he became the most popular guy in school and was elected by his peers to represent them in their convocation.

In most educational and religious practices, the same holds true. Whether we become a mechanic, plumber, mathematician, monk or philosopher, we practice as we learn to be who we want to be in our future. Why not look forward to being part of god rather than backward and repeating our pain and suffering stories from our past?

In the *Bhagavad Gita*, a Hindu scriptural classic, Arjuna, a prince, has a seven hundred verse discussion with Lord Krishna, on the values of life and how to realize that we are Brahman or the Absolute. In chapter seventeen, Krishna talks about something called *shradda*, whose nearest equivalent in English is *faith*.

Shradda literally means "that which is placed in the heart" and includes all of our values, prejudices, perceptions and beliefs. The Gita explains that there is wrong *shradda* – the belief that the world is all there is, and right *shradda*, the belief in our divinity. Life is not passive and pushes us to replace our heartfelt beliefs with the understanding that we are god.[44]

Life is a gestalt of energy creation, life-force drives and inspired interactions. Trust in that and just watch our smoke. Where do we begin and god ends? There is no beginning and no end. We and god are one and the same. Trust that and we will understand that we belong wherever we are because that is what we believe to be true.

We are creating as fast as we can grow. We are learning as fast as we

---

[44] The Bhagavad Gita. 1985. The Blue Mountain Center of Meditation. Canada. 2nd edition.

believe that we can. When we reach out and hold on to the possibility of being god, there are no miracles, just people living their birthrights.

When Babylon fell and there was panic and confusion, people believed that there was great evil committed and they had to straighten their ways. There were those among them even then who believed that the only path to salvation was through suffering.

We suffer because we feel that we must due to guilt, shame, or anger. We then turn our feelings into our reality to legitimize our suffering. What right do we have to only live in the deep and dark side of our egos? We collapse ourselves into self- pity and wait to be struck down by lightning. At same time, we look to the "wicked" with envy. Oh, that we could kick over the traces of life and laugh a little. Life is taken so seriously. Hell rests at every stop. We are the deserving and the undeserving of punishment and salvation. The world takes on shadows of the dark side of our beliefs and rules of behaviour.

In truth, there is only light. Darkness is not the opposite of light but the illusion that light doesn't exist. When we believe there is darkness all around us, we are facing into the dark cave as Plato once said and not the light. We could let go of all of our preconceived notions about reality and simply watch life as it flows and ebbs around us. We could learn to trust in the flow and know that we are a part of life and we belong here.

As we look at life from beginning to end, we can see that we try and fit in at school and at home, find a partner of our dreams, the dream job, the dream life, the dream everything. Dreams are the creative inspirations and palettes of our lives.

Carl Jung said that god speaks to us in our dreams and revelations. As a result of our cultural beliefs, we settle for less than our dreams. Instead, we live our lives of quiet and self-contained frustrations and sorrow. We believe that we will be reunited with our creator and be rewarded for our humility by not demanding anything of ourselves.

We are not meant to be on the earth to be humble about our dreams. We are meant to live. Safety is not alive. Safety is fear. How can we trust that we are *life* if we don't live? Our minds are our storywriters and we believe what we think. In order to understand our god-ness we need to have absolute faith in ourselves, our intuition and our dreams about life. To do this is like stepping off a cliff without a parachute and trusting that we will not crash and burn.

GRACE AND THE VOID

P aul Tillich wrote that grace is twofold: the first form of grace provides direct participation in being to everything. It is the universal energy of being and we don't have to pay for it or earn it. It is life itself. The second form of grace comes to those who feel separated, alone and in deep suffering. It is a gift of forgiveness and of love.[45] This is like two sides of the same coin. Self-forgiveness and self-love come with the grace of being.

In the 1962 movie, *Birdman of Alcatraz*, a fictionalized biography of Robert Stroud (Burt Lancaster) showed how he found grace. Originally he had been imprisoned in Leavenworth for killing a man in Alaska. He was a rebellious and angry young man and in those days, fought the prison system and warden.

He learned that his mother came to visit him but was turned away, and in his anger killed a guard. He was sentenced to death for this but his mother fought so hard to keep him alive that his sentence was commuted to solitary confinement for life.

Imagine being imprisoned for life and how lonely and isolated this would be. One day a wounded bird landed on his window sill and he nursed it back to life. Soon, a trend began and more birds were gifted to Robert and to other prisoners.

Robert went on to become a renowned ornithologist specializing in bird diseases and was described as a genius. He was later transferred to Alcatraz and was refused his birds, due to his continued rebellious nature. Then he stopped a prison riot, saved prisoners' lives and allowed the authorities back into the prison safely. He was never given parole

---

[45] *Tillich, Paul. 1951. "Systematic Theology, Volume 1"*. University of Chicago Press. Chicago, Illinois:USA

but eventually was transferred to a medical facility in Missouri where he died.[46]

In the movie, Stroud discovers compassion and grace through his interaction with his birds. He was considered a psychopath, yet through grace, he added his voice to the harmony of life by his work with birds. Grace can be found in the strangest places.

An Old Testament word for grace is *chesed*. This word speaks of deliverance from enemies, affliction, or adversity through god. It also denotes enablement, daily guidance, forgiveness, and preservation. The New Testament word is *charis*. It focuses on salvation from the void.

We believe that we have to do something to earn grace when it is exactly the opposite. When there is nothing left and we are nothing, we have no pride, no sense of self and no sense in life, there is a quiet sense of forgiveness, peace, love and constancy without any volition. That sense of grace lets us know that we are not alone. We are greater than just our physical self and because there is grace, we can pick up the pieces of our lives and move on. In Hinduism, kripa or divine grace is considered the spiritual key to self-realization or enlightenment.

The void is the opposite of grace and philosophically it is characterized as non-being or emptiness.

Since we are beings, it would seem a contradiction in terms when it is applied to us. Yet, there are people whose lives feel so empty that when they face the void, they can find no reason for living.

I knew someone who had beaten back pancreatic cancer for five years, which is considered a miracle. As Ruth became better, she started dreaming of a fulfilled life in which she was married. Within a year she found her mate, her partner, and they were married. She was filled with joy and happiness. The day after they were married, he told her he had made a mistake and left her. For about a week, her misery was horrendous. Within a month her cancer came back and she died within three months.

When people encounter the void, life feels empty, hopeless and useless. At those times, it is hard to believe that the void, that emptiness, is our greatest construct and has locked the door to grace. Ironically, when we

---

[46] Wikipedia.2012. Birdman of Alcatraz (film). Modified March 2017. https://en.wikipedia.org/wiki/Birdman_of_Alcatraz_(film)

accept that same emptiness and allow the door to open, we discover our divinity through grace.

As we move through life, we don't consider such weighty things often. We are on a trajectory to prove ourselves and make our way in the world. Sure, we have our bumps, but we know that just around the corner everything will be all right. We will get that perfect job, perfect partner and perfect life. For a while that is true, then a little tarnish happens. Perhaps it is the first gray hair or our child not doing well in school or becoming an addict. Maybe we just get bored with happiness and wonder if that is all there is to life. After a while, all the stuff in the world is not that attractive yet the yearning for something more continues. That is when we start to question what that more is. We ask, "If life is not stuff, then what? If life is not relationships, then what?"

When the yearning becomes strong enough, we become seekers and feel that somehow, when we discover the meaning of life, all will be well.

That yearning is the quest for our own divinity, for our own understanding of all that is. We are hungry to feel part of that wholeness of being and we first attempt to quell that feeling with known rituals. We seek advice from friends and relatives. We speak to counsellors about our dissatisfaction with life. We search out various religions, trying them on like a pair of pants to see if there is a fit for us. If we are very lucky, we may find our way early on. We get an epiphany about life and settle down in contentment. If we are not so lucky, we continue to yearn and suffer, not knowing if there is something "out there" that can help us in our search.

As we look, either we become more embittered and cynical or we open our hearts to the wonder of living. What helps us to open our hearts is grace. It is ours, we can keep it and we can share it. The problem is that the feeling of grace is hard to hold on to. We try to. It feels so good. But it is a fleeting feeling and we use memory to reinforce with ourselves how good grace feels. Then we continue to be seekers. The purpose of the seeking this time is to understand what grace is and how we are part of it.

Without the yearning towards the mystery of life and death, the yearning for the connection to god, life would be pretty empty. It feels like facing a void where there is no hope or meaning in the world.

Seekers vary in religion, walks of life, values and employment. There is not one trauma that creates the sense of emptiness. It could be from a cumulative effect of a disappointing life, a drive that has always been there or an illness or sorrow that doesn't abate.

The seeking begins when a person looks out into the world and asks, "Is this all there is?" The answer in our scientific and reasoning culture is, "Yes, this is it."

In our world, love, sex, wealth, knowledge and power are touted as signs of success. Unethical business practices are good because we get wealthy. It is about screwing the other guy so we can get ahead.

We are facing a world of increasing population and decreasing hope. We are experiencing unprecedented problems such as pollution and global warming, but like the characters in Edgar Allen Poe's story, *The Masque of the Red Death*, we hide ourselves behind locked doors in the hope that this will pass us by.

The void is created by our misunderstanding that we are alone and separate in the world. The void is our feelings of emptiness and loss of hope that there is purpose and meaning in life. The void is the lack of caring for each other in fundamental ways such as community and compassion and instead believing in self above all. The void is about non-being and is a human belief construct in contradiction of being.

Since we are the human part of being, there is hope. We can see hope in movies where our hero is kind, helpful and honest. They are today's mythology and religion. We want to exemplify our leaders and actors who show us the qualities of integrity, honesty and hope.

Hope is about how we can conquer life's difficulties. We are not alone and there is love and caring in the world. Life has a purpose because we are part of it. We can easily use our dreams and unconscious interface to talk to god whenever we want and create the conversation into our physical world. The world of being-itself and the world of humanity are two sides of the same coin and we can be with grace when we let go of our fear of the void.

In life there is suffering but there is also hope. All it requires is that we believe in ourselves and get to know who we are. Not our stories and beliefs of who we are but the "who" we are in our dreams of life.

Our conscious ability to daydream is a reflection of creation.
Trust yourself! Take the risk and slide on the ice.

HOME FREE

Here we are at the end of my book. It has been an incredible journey from being curious about our relationship to god to understanding that we are god. At first, saying we are god was disconcerting. It sounded like I was saying that we are in control of life. What we are in control of is our perceptions, our stories, our fears, our dreams and our actions in the world.

It is amazing that our brainwave frequencies match our planet's frequency and every night we have to go through those brainwaves to sleep and to wake up in the morning. Our experience of a three-dimensional reality is more dream-like than we thought.

The science of quantum mechanics sounds like science fiction and confirms that our world as we know it is deeply personal. We think that everything we see is solid and real, when actually, with a change in our perception, the world changes. Quantum mechanics shows our reality to be fluid, self-governing and all-encompassing.

There is a theory called Many Worlds or the Everett Interpretation[47], developed by Burt Everett in 1957 and popularized by Brett Seligman in the 1960's and 1970's to explain Schrodinger's cat dilemma where the cat is in a cage with radioactive material, hydrocyanic acid and a Geiger counter. The cat is simultaneously alive and dead until an impersonal observer looks at the situation of whether or not the radioactive material decays, sets off the Geiger counter and releases the hydrocyanic acid, or not. Schrodinger used this as an example of how ridiculous quantum mechanics appears to be.

---

[47] Wikipedia. 2017. "Many-worlds Interpretation." Last modified September 24, 2017. https://en.wikipedia.org/wiki/Many-worlds_interpretation

The Many Worlds theory makes quantum mechanics weirder because Seligman and Everett mathematically proved that the cat could simultaneously be alive and dead - by becoming part of a different world. They postulated that every time we make a decision or create a belief about life, we split from the world we are in to one that is compatible with our beliefs. Incredible sounding as this theory is, it has been proven to be mathematically correct. Life is stranger than fiction.

Richard Bach wrote a book called *One*, where he described a fictionalized account of his wife, Leslie, and himself on a journey, travelling to different worlds as they made decisions about their past and future. Even though it read like a science-fiction novel, his information came from the science of quantum mechanics. Leslie and Richard's conclusion at the end of the novel is also the title of the book, *One*.

We are all one. We are all part of a quantum sea, rippling through each other's lives, interacting with all of the infinite ripples that intersect with ours. No wonder we don't have complete control of our own lives. We are not alone, separate and suffering the slings and arrows of an uncaring god. We are all together in a universal sea of possibility and energy.

Think of the times when something terrible could have occurred but a miracle occurred and changed the probable ending.

I have a friend who should have drowned and he didn't. Jack was backing his truck onto a ramp into the river to get his boat out of the water. Suddenly the parking brake let go and the truck pushed him deeper and under the water. Now Jack can't swim, and he wasn't wearing a life preserver. While he was underwater, he was amazed he could open his eyes and see his truck under water and he was also surprised that he could float. He floated to the box of his truck (which was underwater) and hung on. He was in the water for over two hours before the ambulance and police came to rescue him. They called a tow truck, which towed his truck and boat out of the water and took him and his vehicles home.

The shock of the experience and the cold of the water created hypothermia and while lying shivering in his bed, he had a heart attack.

No, the story isn't finished yet. His wife called for an ambulance, which was late in getting there because all the ambulances were on call outs. When he was driven to the hospital hours later and he checked over, Jack was given a clean bill of health. How could all of this have occurred?

It was a miracle that when the truck pushed Jack underwater he didn't drown. It was a miracle that he floated to the back of his truck. It was a miracle that he saved his boat. It was a miracle that he didn't die from hypothermia or a heart attack and it was a miracle that he is now at home, living his life, not feeling as though any miracle had occurred at all.

Miracles in our world are the ripples of the quantum sea intersecting with each other. Being an I of god, our actions, beliefs, personal history, drives and dreams interact with all the other parts of god, not out there, but everywhere throughout the vibrating frequencies and quantum fields of all-that-is.

Our conscious ability to daydream, have drives, tell stories, remember our histories, have personal, spiritual and cultural views of the world, is a reflection of creation at the primordial level.

When I speak of quantum mechanics and vibrating quantum fields as being the ground of all existence, I include consciousness. We think that we are the only species that learns, dreams and has memories, but all of life, including bugs, trees and subatomic particles have consciousness. Consciousness includes our collective unconscious, our subconscious, our dreams and our drives.

In the old days of classical mechanics (or three-dimensional reality), scientists believed that thinking was created by neurons in our brains. Candace Pert came along with her book, *The Molecules of Emotion*, and proved that thinking was done throughout our bodies by biochemical molecules. Molecules are made up of atoms and the nucleus of the atom is made up of quantum particles. Our bodies are in the circle of life.

When we are asleep and dreaming, we are comfortable with a fluid reality. In our dreams we fly, shift time, talk to fairies, dead relatives, and future children. We travel to different worlds, do different jobs, have different ages and bodies, even change gender at times. We don't question our dreams. It is a natural part of life and in fact we need to dream. If we don't sleep and dream, in time, we start hallucinating in our three-dimensional, conscious world.

What is real? Our sleeping, dream-state or our awake, conscious world of classical mechanics? Mind-body healing, psychoneuroimmunology, hypnotherapy, acupuncture, placebos, psychiatry and all other non-medicinal healing methods rely more on our theta and delta brainwaves (sleeping) than they do on our alpha and beta brainwaves (awake and aware).

When we use those modalities, we are using our theta brainwaves while we are awake, thus combining our sleeping and waking consciousness and creating change in our lives. As we practice meditating, creative visualization, mindfulness, painting, writing, self-hypnosis, et cetera, we increase our awareness of reality outside of classical mechanics and utilize our unity with the quantum sea of possibility.

Each of us is an I of god. Being everything is not a mental construct. It is scientific fact. However, as unrealistic as quantum mechanics appears to be, on the most basic level, we are one in the creation of life, the universe, and the ground of all existence.

These are not religious or philosophical ideas. Life as we know it is not a three-dimensional reality but an illusion at its core. This is hard for us to swallow as our world seems so real.

We are more comfortable creating a god out there who is in charge of life, death and grace, than accepting that we are god creating our world with its life, death and grace.

We are stardust and we are our dreams.

When we are despondent, we think that we should just let go of striving to do things right and see what happens next. Why do we try so hard to be somebody? Why must we suffer so much in an effort to be perfect? Why can't someone just love us for who we are, not for who they want us to be? Why not? Perhaps that is the truth we are unaware of. What would happen if we stopped trying to fit in with all the rules of success and happiness? Maybe we would develop wisdom and self-acceptance.

When we look out of our window, we can see everything outside but we know we cannot touch it or feel it because there is a window between us and the outdoors. In the same way, we have a window to the infinite that we can see in our dreams, but our minds create the illusion that we are separate and cannot experience it. How can we break the window and create a door to freedom?

First of all, we throw away all the rules about our beliefs, our histories and our habits. We question everything that we think is real and everything that we believe is not real.

I can remember sitting on our couch one day when I realized that

I could do anything I wanted at any time of the day. I could eat what I wanted, sleep when I wanted, sit and watch television all day if I wanted, believe what I wanted, wear what I wanted and behave how I wanted, provided I did nobody else any harm.

Having no rules is fun because my only guidelines are the ones I choose. Whenever I decide to do something different that frightens me, I remind myself that there are no rules that say I can't do it.

I signed up for a yoga course and as I was getting ready to go, I was insecure about my age (older), my appearance (flabby) and my level of skill (beginner). I had no yoga pants, only cut off leggings, my yoga mat was old and I didn't know if I would fit in. Normally those feelings stopped me and I would not go and try something new. This time, I reminded myself that there were no rules about age, dress, skill or appearance. Did I want to go? You bet! In the end, I had a wonderful yoga session and I will go back for more.

Patience is required to bring change into our lives. Remember the discussion on chaos theory and little whirlpools of energy? When we make decisions, it takes time, a lot of time for the chaotic whirlpools of energy to coalesce into one big whirlpool or change. As well, since we are part of infinity, entanglement in our environment and lives (like the ripples on a pond) affect our changes and we have to have faith in what we are changing.

In a culture where self-repair is big business, faith in ourselves is difficult. Our inner voices usually tell us how we cannot do what we want and how undeserving we are of success. Faith in ourselves is key. In this case, if our faith wavers, we fake it until we learn to have faith in ourselves through successful, small steps in how we feel.

Pick a dream you are afraid you can't fulfill and commit to making it work. Don't worry about a time frame until you are ready. Walk the steps every day mentally, emotionally and creatively. When you go to sleep at night, dream about what you want to do. There will be roadblocks, disappointments, successes and self-discovery along the path of your dream. It is in our commitment to the creation of our dreams that we utilize both sides of our brains, both sides of our realities and all of infinity.

Nobody can tell us how to experience our lives or god. Nobody runs us or controls us. We get to choose what we want, how we live and what we think and believe. Life is our palette to do our greatest work and our grandest dreams.

J. Krishnamurti was a spiritual teacher who taught that thinking created our sense of self. Our memories, opinions, beliefs and stories colour everything we look at, he said. Krishnamurti suggested that the opposite of not living in our minds would be the art of living.[48]

There is no guarantee of our longevity in this life. We are part of the energetic sea of everything and since all of the ripples of our thoughts, actions and dreams interact with the other infinite ripples of everything, who knows which part of infinity we are journeying to next. Carpe diem! Seize the day! Step outside your comfort zone, your safe reality box with all of your rules about who you are. Trust yourself, take the risk and slide on the ice! We are all god.

Trust yourself, take the risk and slide on the ice! We are all god.

---

[48] Krishamurti Foundation Trust, Ltd. *Krishnamurti Reader.* Shambala Publications Inc, 2011

From the Sutra Of Hui Neng
The Basic Scripture of Zen Buddhism

If we are treading the Path of Enlightenment
We need not be worried by stumbling-blocks.
Provided we keep a constant eye on our own faults
We cannot go astray from the right path.
Since every species of life has its own way to salvation
They will not interfere with or be antagonistic to one another.
But if we leave our own path and seek some other way of salvation
We shall not find it,
And though we plod on till death overtakes us
We shall only find penitence in the end.

He who treads the Path in earnest
Sees not the mistakes of the world;
If we find fault with others
We ourselves are also in the wrong.

When neither hatred nor love disturb our mind
Serenely we sleep.

When the disciple is free from all doubts
It indicates that his Essence of Mind has been found.

To seek enlightenment by separating from this world
Is as absurd as to search for a rabbit's horn.
Right views are called 'transcendental'
Erroneous views are called 'worldly'.

When all views, right or erroneous are discarded
Then the essence of Bodhi appears.

Kalpa after kalpa a man may be under delusion
But once enlightened it takes him only a minute to attain Buddhahood.[49]

---

[49] The Sutra Of Hui Neng. Fourth edition 1966.The Buddhist Society. London. S.W.1. England. Pages 40-41.

BIBLIOGRAPHY

Armstrong, Karen. 2003. *The History Of God*, alt.binaries.e-book.palm (PDB-PIC-TXT Bundle) and (UBook). http://www.metaphysicspirit.com/books/A%20History%20of%20God.pdf

Barr, Stephen M. 2012. *Does Quantum Physics Make It Easier to Believe In God?* https://www.bigquestionsonline.com/2012/07/10/does-quantum-physics-make-easier-believe-god

Bendetti, F. 2002. *All in The Mind*. Economist, 362 (8261), 83-85

Brennan, Barbara A. 1988. *Hands of Light*. Bantam Books New York, NY USA. 19-56

Bryce Seligman DeWitt, *Quantum Mechanics and Reality: Could the solution to the dilemma of indeterminism be a universe in which all possible outcomes of an experiment actually occur?* Physics Today, 23(9) pp 30–40 (September 1970) "every quantum transition taking place on every star, in every galaxy, in every remote corner of the universe is splitting our local world on earth into myriads of copies of itself." See also Physics Today, letters follow up, 24(4), (April 1971), pp 38–44

Dacher, E. 1991. *PNI-The New Mind/Body Healing Program*. Paragon House. New York, NY: USA

Emerick, Y. 2008. *Rumi Meditations. The Complete Idiot's Guide to*. Special Markets, Alpha Books, Hudson, NY. USA. 134

Frankl, Victor 1984. *Man's Search for Meaning*. Pocket Books, Simon & Shuster. New York, NY: USA. 21-113

How 40,000 Tons of Cosmic Dust Falling to Earth Affects You and Me. http://news.nationalgeographic.com/ 2015/01/150128-big-bang-universe-supernova-astrophysics-health-space-ngbooktalk/ January 28, 2015

Jung, Carl G. 1965. *Man and His Symbols*. Dell Publishing, New York, NY: USA, 3-94

J. Krishnamurti, 2011. *The Krishnamurti Reader*. Shambala Publications. Boston, Massachusetts. USA. 1-5

Levine, Stephen. 2002. *Turning Toward the Mystery*. Harper Collins Publishers, New York, NY: USA, 10-11

McLellan, J., Dorn, H.1999. *Science and Technology in World History*, Johns Hopkins University, Baltimore, MD, USA: 246-273

Mindful. *Getting Started with Mindfulness*. http://www.mindful.org/ meditation/mindfulness-getting-started/

Mystical Blaze. *Seth on Life After Death and The Soul*. http://www. mysticalblaze.com/ProphetsSethLOD.htm

Nuland, S. 2001. *The Uncertain Art*, American Scholar, 70 (3), 123-127

Pappas, Stephanie. 2012. *Early Neglect Alters Kids' Brains*. Live Science. Accessed March 11, 2017. http://www.livescience.com/21778-early-neglect-alters-kids-brains.html

Roberts, Jane. 2001. *The Seth Material*. http://www.afterlifedata.com/life-after-death-topics-140-1-Who-or-what-is-God.html

Talbot, M. 1991. *The Holographic Universe*. HarperCollins Publishers. New York. NY: USA

The Bhagavad Gita. 1985. The Blue Mountain Center of Meditation. Canada. 2nd edition. 57-58. 243-249

The Diamond Sutra. 2001. Red Pine. Counterpoint. Berkeley, CA. USA Dist. ByPublishers Group West. 2-3 Proverbs, chapter 16;1-4, 8-9

The Naked Scientists. August 24, 2015. https://www.thenakedscientists.com/articles/interviews/one-theory-rule-them-all..

The Sutra of Hui Neng. 1966. Translated by Wong Mou-Lam. The Buddhist Society. London, England. S.W.1, 41-42

Tillich, Paul. 1951. *Systematic Theology, Volume One.* University of Chicago Press, Chicago, Illinois. 211-289

Wikipedia. 2017. *Advaita Vedanta.* Last modified February 9, 2017. https://en.wikipedia.org/wiki/Advaita_Vedanta

Wikipedia. 2006. *Agapism.* Last modified November 14, 2016. https://en.wikipedia.org/wiki/Agapism

Wikipedia. 2016. *Atoms.* Last modified September 11, 2017. https://en.wikipedia.org/wiki/Atom

Wikipedia. 2012. *Birdman of Alcatraz* (film). Last modified March 2017. https://en.wikipedia.org/wiki/Birdman_of_Alcatraz_(film)

Wikipedia. 2017. *God is Dead.* Last modified July 7, 2017. https://en.wikipedia.org/wiki/God_is_deadWikipedia. 2016.

Wikipedia. 2017. *Guru.* Last modified March 31, 2017. https://en.wikipedia.org/wiki/Guru

Wikipedia. 2016. *Hinduism.* Last modified February 23, 2017. https://en.wikipedia.org/wiki/Hinduism

Wikipedia. 2017. *History of Atheism.* Last modified February 13, 2017. https://en.wikipedia.org/wiki/History_of_atheism

Wikipedia. 2016. *History of Religion.* Last modified May 17, 2017. https://en.wikipedia.org/wiki/History_of_religions

Wikipedia. 2017. *Holocaust.* Last modified February 20, 2017.en.wikipedia.org/w/index.php?title=The_Holocaust&action=history

Wikipedia. 2006. *Kundalini.* Last modified June 1, 2017. https://en.wikipedia.org/wiki/Kundalini

Wikipedia. 2016. *Many Worlds Interpretation.* Last modified June 9, 2017. https://en.wikipedia.org/wiki/Many-worlds_interpretation

Wikipedia. 2017. *Maslow's hierarchy of needs.* Last modified March 20, 2017. https://en.wikipedia.org/wiki/Maslow%27s_hierarchy_of_needs

Wikipedia, 2016. *Mettā.* Last modified May 5, 2017. https://en.wikipedia.org/wiki/Mett%C4%81

Wikipedia. 2016. *Mysticism.* Last modified June 18, 2017. https://en.wikipedia.org/w/index.php?title=Mysticism&action=history

Wikipedia. 2016.*Nisargadatta Maharaj.* Last modified March 6, 2017. https://en.wikipedia.org/wiki/Nisargadatta_Maharaj

Wikipedia. 2016. *Noah's Ark.* Last modified January 20, 2017https://en.wikipedia.org/w/index.php?title=Noah%27s_Ark&action=history

Wikipedia. 2015. *Now I Lay Me Down To Sleep.* Last modified January 16, 2017. https://en.wikipedia.org/wiki/Now_I_Lay_Me_Down_to_Sleep

Wikipedia. 2015. *Paleolithic Religion.* Last modified February 8, 2017. https://en.wikipedia.org/wiki/Paleolithic_religion

Wikipedia. 2016. *Schrodinger's Cat.* Last modified October 23, 2017. https://en.wikipedia.org/wiki/Schr%C3%B6dinger%27s_cat

Wikipedia. 2017. *Theosis.* 2014. Last modified May 4, 2017. https://en.wikipedia.org/wiki/Theosis_(Eastern_Christian_theology)

Wikipedia. 2006. *Wine Of The Dreamers.* Last modified December 27, 2016. https://en.wikipedia.org/wiki/Wine_of_the_Dreamers